The 7 Pillars

of

Habit Building

and

Self-Discipline

67 Habits to Develop Focus, Sharpen
Concentration, and Beat Laziness. Achieve
Your Goals and Be More Successful by
Mastering the Art of Self-Control

NEIL KRISTOFF COOPER

Table of Contents

Introduction

In an ever busy, fast-paced world, it's sometimes hard to keep track of your daily actions. And when you do, you might not do it effectively, or to the best of your abilities. You know that there is a wide world of opportunities out there, and maybe your dream is to achieve your greatest goals. However, perhaps bad habits, like procrastination and spending excessive time on social media, are holding you back, hindering you from the dreams you wish every day to accomplish.

But it doesn't have to be like this. You don't have to stay in the rut of bad habits forever, and deep down, you know it. All you have to do is learn how to flex your self-discipline muscles and form better habits, master your focus to help you reach your full potential.

Indeed, breaking bad habits and forming new ones can be tricky. In some sense, it's not because you don't want to break them. The truth is, that this is just how the brain works. Humans are built to react to stimuli and anticipate the results of their actions. The brain develops an expectation that it will receive rewards in a specific manner, under specific conditions, which is how habits are formed. Your brain will constantly remind you to behave in a certain way in response to certain stimuli, based on how you initially reacted to them.

Still, this doesn't mean we don't have the control to form new habits, right? This is where self-discipline comes in. It's your brain, after all, and you have to take life by the reins and wield your actions in the way they ought to be.

There are several reasons why overcoming bad habits is so challenging, but one thing is for sure; it takes a lot of determination to stop negative behavioral patterns and avoid them.

In this book, I will share with you the 7 pillars of Habit Building and Self-Discipline that can shape your life—not just for a couple of weeks but for a lifetime. You'll find not only the science behind the theories but also strategies and practical advice that you can readily apply in your daily activities, how you can master your focus, as well as get rid of procrastination.

Over the years as a productivity coach, I've worked with hundreds of different people preoccupied with different levels of busyness. But if they have one thing in common, it's the fact that all of them are challenged to deliver their preferred output.

Seeing them transform from being frustrated and stuck, to consistently hitting their goals by applying these strategies, brings me tremendous satisfaction and joy.

As a previous manager who spent a great number of years in corporate America, I saw a lot of my employees struggle with their concentration due to constant interruptions left, right, and center. At one point, I used to struggle with these myself, causing me to miss targets and opportunities.

Applying these powerful strategies have helped me get back on track. And now, I'm also sharing what I learned.

The ability to control your conduct allows you to select and adhere to actions, attitudes, and behaviors that promote growth and success. Additionally, it offers you the willpower and inner fortitude you need to get rid of your unhealthy habits, avoid procrastination and laziness, and complete your tasks.

Our habits begin to happen automatically once they are learned, practiced, and acquired. We learned how to do things like brush our teeth and drive a car through a sequence of processes that needed a lot of focus and time, but today we do them automatically. We rely on habits a lot because they enable us to complete multiple tasks in daily life, often while simultaneously completing other tasks, without having to pause and give our full attention to one task at a time. This saves us time and energy. Sounds great, doesn't it? The main drawback is that creating healthy habits requires effort and consideration. Thankfully, science provides advice on where to start as well as methods to make your life smoother.

This book takes on a holistic approach and guarantees to give you an understanding on how the different facets of your existence affect your self-discipline. And how, in turn, it affects how you build stronger and newer habits that make you a better you.

The first four chapters will talk about the fundamentals of habit formation and the different areas of your life that play a key role in building a lasting one. The last three will talk more about the 'how' and will provide you with different processes and strategies, as well as actionable guides that you can follow.

The techniques that I've shared in this book have helped me to make my dream of having a coaching business become a reality. Therefore, my end goal is to help you cultivate healthy, habitual behaviors that will help you strengthen your self-discipline and achieve personal success, too.

Habits are important for such success, because they have a significant impact on how we feel, act, and think, which pretty much encompasses all we do. We develop thought, action, and emotional routines, and this makes up most, if not all, of our lives. In reality, after we've made a decision to pursue a goal, our daily motivation is often derived from the habits we've established to help us succeed.

So, if you want to achieve something remarkable but can't break through and don't know how to make it happen, this book will serve as a blueprint on how to get there.

As individuals, we are the only ones capable of changing our lives. Although we might get advice, support and a plethora of outside help, it all comes down to us in the end, what we do and how we do it. The easiest route for change and improvement is to adjust the things you do every day. Being stuck in a vicious cycle of failure, mistakes, and disappointment doesn't have to be your story forever, and this book will help you take the first step. The rest is entirely in your hands.

The techniques and strategies you're about to read are proven to yield incredible results for busy people living in various kinds of family dynamics. Each chapter in this book will outline a pillar that greatly affects your daily productivity as well as strategies on how to implement them in your personal life.

So, what are you waiting for? Let's dive into your guide to a bigger and brighter future through healthy habit formations, and grounding yourself in self-discipline.

Pillar 1:

Foundation

Perhaps we've all heard, at least once in our lives, that if we want to master something, we must know it first. For us to fully grasp the concept of building healthy habits and establishing ourselves in keen, upright self-discipline, the first thing to do is getting a deeper grasp of what it is, so we can tackle it from the outside. Sounds just about practical, wouldn't you agree?

So, in this section, we dive into learning more about habits and self-discipline in a way that you've probably never noticed before.

The Truth About Habits and Self-Discipline

So, what exactly are habits, and what do these have to do with self-discipline?

What Are Habits?

Habits can be regarded as behaviors brought on by an internal or external impulse that happens routinely. Hence, it's anything you frequently and consistently do, perhaps without realizing it.

One person might, for instance, have a habit of tapping their feet or biting the end of a pen or pencil. Perhaps someone else always brushes their teeth before going to bed. Basically, something that is repeated often enough to become habitual might be deemed a habit. You don't really need to consider doing it any more. It simply occurs.

We could argue that our habits determine how successful we are in life. And in some sense, this might be true, here's how:

The routine actions we take, shape who we are and the outcomes we produce. Because of this, developing healthy habits and eliminating bad ones is a vital life skill with numerous advantages.

Habits of the mind is another outlook on habits. This viewpoint emphasizes our aims more than our actions, which are directly related to our self-discipline. It involves making wise decisions when faced with issues, indecision, or uncertainty. We should use our mental resources to accomplish this. Basically, our mental habits are what enable us to embark on successful actions that lead to achievements over the long run. Cultivating these habits to reach your goals is the ultimate goal with this book.

Healthy Habits

Our interests in habits are usually to break bad ones and form healthy ones; so identifying our good habits is the ideal place to start.

Below are a few examples of healthy behaviors you can develop or maintain

- exercising regularly

- drinking eight glasses of water each day

- sleeping for seven to eight hours every night

- journaling

- switching off your phone before going to bed every night

- using affirmations in the morning

- cultivating good nutritional habits

- taking time to self-reflect

- limiting social media use

- making use of self-compassion

- practicing daily meditation

Bad Habits

Good habits, and how to form them, has always been a relatively easy topic to explore. But how about kicking unhealthy habits to the curb? The advantage (and disadvantage) of habits is that they become automatic once they are practiced frequently. This is fantastic for positive habits, but it also contributes to how challenging it is to eradicate negative ones.

It's probably more difficult to break an existing habit than it is to form a new one. Examples of such habits include smoking, gambling, drinking, overeating or binging unhealthy foods, and squandering time and money.

Just about anything you do routinely that puts you at a disadvantage is a bad habit, whether we accept it or not. So, does procrastination qualify as a bad habit? There are sources that claim that there is some 'good' in procrastination, but as long as it causes a damper on your day and productivity, then it's a bad habit (Newsonen, 2015).

Another pesky little thing about bad habits is the risk of swapping one bad habit for another. The fact is that if we reward ourselves for positive habits, it works as an incentive for us to strengthen them.

Well, in the same way, harmful habits also provide rewards, which is often why we continue to have them and why they become so strong. Perhaps overeating chocolate every night makes us feel good. Or maybe over-spending allows us to feel comfortable in whatever commodity we buy.

But often, when we stop one bad habit and can't find another means to obtain the advantage presented by that habit, we just resume a new bad habit. For instance, a person could give up drinking and start doing drugs. Or someone might quit eating ice cream and begin eating an excessive amount of cookies.

The truth is, emotions are the cornerstone of bad habits. Therefore, if we don't substitute bad habits with better ones that fulfill equivalent needs, we risk swapping habits in search of the 'feeling' that emerges from doing so.

So, how exactly do you break a bad habit?

Finding a healthy behavior that provides you with a similar incentive to your unhealthy habit is one of the most useful techniques for quitting bad habits.

For example, you may write in your gratitude journal instead of binge watching a TV show. Or, if you're attempting to cut back on drinking, choose a different enjoyable evening activity that you'll still love. The objective is to switch out the bad habit for one that you'll genuinely appreciate equally as much as the bad one.

What Is Self-Discipline?

Self-discipline is the capacity to exert self-control and force oneself to work hard or act in a specific manner without the assistance of another person.

It's the ability to accomplish what you want to do, not the ability to follow orders from others. It involves being able to control your feelings, ideas, and conduct in order to accomplish your objectives. When defined and analyzed in this manner, self-discipline projects a variety of favorable results.

Focus and self-control lead to satisfaction, contentment, and success. When faced with all the alluring temptations of bad habits and bad decisions, it can be hard to resist. But the fact is that those with self-discipline are happier (Sasson, n.d). Why? Because when we exercise self-control and discipline, we actually achieve more of the things that are most important to us. It's the link between goals set and goals achieved.

Here are a few examples of exercising self-discipline in everyday life:

- **The power of resistance.** Individuals who are self-disciplined have the ability to get rid of all traces of temptation from their lives. That also applies to interruptions. To put your cell phone away and concentrate on the task at hand, or to switch off the TV show and redirect your attention to what is necessary, takes a lot of self-discipline.

- **The ability to forgive.** It's never easy to let go of something that truly wounded you. The ability to put a situation in the past, so you and a coworker or team member can effectively work on a project or task, takes self-discipline and self-control.

- **The ability to adapt to a situation.** Self-discipline helps us to easily and effectively adapt to any situation, even when we are not prepared to do so. For instance, if you have a presentation for work and your computer crashes, self-discipline will allow you to effectively handle the situation, instead of panicking or showing frustration.

- **Time management.** Knowing how to manage your time effectively is an essential component of productivity; you can complete any task with satisfaction and in a time-efficient manner. You have the strength and time-management skills to complete everything on your to-do list.

- **Physical exercise.** A genuine act of self-discipline is the capacity to decide to work out and prioritize fitness and health while you could be participating in other fun activities.

- **Following through.** Following through with good behaviors and habits every day means you're right on track, and it might just be the most ideal example of self-discipline.

You may want to change your lifestyle to strengthen your self-discipline, which might be inconvenient and occasionally uncomfortable. Habits often drive our decisions instead of the actual process of decision-making, making it challenging to overcome bad habits. You'll have a higher chance of changing negative habits and forming new, healthy ones if you shake things up a little. This is just the beginning.

Why Are They Important to Master?

Contrary to popular understanding, developing self-discipline doesn't mean being hard on yourself or having a restricted lifestyle. And having healthy habits doesn't mean your life has to be mundane without a moment of thrill.

It just means you're more equipped to tackle everything life throws at you, and, more importantly, reap the benefits they yield.

Why Are Habits Important?

Creating habits requires time and work. You'll need planning, responsibility, tenacity, patience, and other traits to succeed, and you'll also encounter challenges like laziness, procrastination, and stress. Therefore, it should come as no surprise that often people give up too soon, while the majority are completely unaware of their habits.

So what's truly in it for you with all this habit talk? And why should you even bother with it at all? In addition to feeling successful, improving self-discipline, and being more deliberate with your thoughts and deeds, here are five more benefits of creating good habits.

You Can Achieve Your Goals and Be More Productive

Big goals and ambitious aspirations don't materialize overnight. The good news is that habits can be helpful in this situation because they are actions that become automatic, reliable, and less challenging for you. When you have good habits, you're more effective, productive, and strategic about the ideas and practices that move you closer to your objectives.

For example, saying you would like to save a thousand dollars by December might sound difficult. But saving a dollar a day might just be the good habit you need to reach this goal.

You Can Become the Person You Most Want to Be

Consider all the accomplished authors, CEOs, and businesspeople you know. They probably didn't become the best in their fields quickly or easily. And I'll bet they continue to show up day in and day out even when they're unmotivated, have difficulties, or just don't "feel like it".

It can be far simpler to become the person you really want to be if you establish routines and habits that support you, rather than relying on sudden surges of motivation.

You Influence Others Around You

If you're a parent, you'll notice that your children often imitate your mannerisms and speech patterns. Couples eventually adopt each other's relationship patterns and even begin to speak, think, and act in similar ways. Consider the traits and customs that sports teams, towns, cultures, and even entire nations have in common.

There is no doubt that the things you do on a regular basis affect others around you. Forming the proper habits is a great approach to setting an example or influencing others.

The Appropriate Habits Improve Your Life's Overall Quality

Keystone habits are those behaviors that have the potential to influence multiple facets of your life. These have links with other constructive behaviors, so success in one area may have an impact on others. Consider exercise as an example, which not only promotes health and fitness but also increases productivity, time management, energy management, mental wellbeing, and more.

Additionally, when two or more habits are combined, routines are formed—morning routines, afternoon routines, night-time routines, weekend routines—and it's these patterns that make us more effective and enable us to consistently have days that are very productive.

You Can Benefit from Good Habits for The Rest of Your Life

Because of habits, all the advantages previously mentioned won't be one-time events. Since habits are whatever you do repeatedly, you get to keep achieving your goals, becoming the person you really want to be, assisting those around you, and improving the quality of your life in general.

You'll feel more accomplished, develop self-discipline, and be more intentional due to good habits. You get to enjoy these advantages for years and years to come.

Why Is Self-Discipline Important?

Self-discipline is a life skill. You can use this skill to make decisions and follow through on them without having to reconsider. As a result, it's an essential requirement for completing activities and attaining goals.

A person who practices discipline is more reliable when it comes to their time, has a habit of perseverance, and is more likely to take charge of their lives. Such a person can make plans and take actions to reach their goals.

You can benefit from discipline in many aspects of your life. Maintaining self-discipline would help you to

- avoid making hasty, impulsive decisions.

- make sensible, healthy decisions.

- keep the promises and commitments you've made to others as well as to yourself.

- get over your propensity for procrastinating and being lazy.

- keep working on the project, even when you don't want to.

- work out, take a walk, or visit the gym.

- maintain your diet plan and avoid giving in to the need to eat unhealthy food.

- remove bad habits.

- attain the willpower to quickly get out of bed in the morning, regardless of how tired you are.

- increase your capacity for sustained attention when working, reading, or learning.

- easily complete your chores and pursue your objectives assid-uously.

Achieving even a little portion of this list is a fantastic accomplishment that can improve your life.

Lack Of Self-Discipline

A lack of self-discipline can result in failure, loss, relationship deterioration, health issues, obesity, and dissatisfaction.

These are a few specific examples of what a lack of self-discipline can do:

- When you're attempting to lose weight, you may not be able to stop yourself from eating something fattening.

- You may occasionally act rashly or in the heat of the moment, hurting the people you care about.

- You could develop a social media addiction that prevents you from putting your phone down for a short period of time.

- You won't be able to follow through on your plans or implement your decisions.

- You may have uncontrollable anger.

- You may lack the willpower to reduce couch time and start exercising, you risk harming your health.

The majority of individuals understand the value of discipline, but few actually take action to enhance it. However, just like every other skill, self-discipline can be improved.

You can use this talent to sit down and study, work out physically, or learn new skills. Additionally, it can aid in meditation, spiritual development, and self-improvement.

Putting These Together for Life

Anything worth achieving takes time to manifest. What matters most is the things you do consistently, regularly, and habitually on a daily basis, not occasionally. This implies that it will require time and work from you.

When paired with goal-setting, enthusiasm, and planning, self-discipline becomes incredibly effective. Ensure that you do everything in your ability to adhere to your goals by writing them down. Before beginning another task, always finish the one you've already started.

Powerful Elements of Self-Discipline

We know the core meaning of self-discipline, its importance and its relationship to habits. But what are the core elements that actually make up self-discipline? There are seven major elements of self-discipline, defined here:

1. **Motivation & desires**: The driving force behind your self-control; the long-term objectives you aim for.

2. **Emotions**: Mental state evoked by a mood, situation or circumstance.

3. **Fear**: A human emotion that typically indicates a danger or threat.

4. **Intellect**: Your ability to reason and understand.

5. **Self-Confidence**: A state of being clear-headed and driven toward a certain goal.

6. **Monitoring**: Being conscious of and keeping track of your actions and emotions.

7. **Willpower**: Your capacity to control your conduct.

These elements are in different degrees of conflict in every human. Sometimes our **intellect** pulls us in one direction while our **emotions** pull us in another. Or, our **desires and motivation** try to guide us in a certain direction, but our **fears** prevent us from going there.

Take, for instance, a scenario where you're being sent to another country for business, lasting for a year. You may have family at home, but you know it's a great opportunity. Your rational mind will probably contradict your emotional mind, stirring internal conflict. In the same way, your desire to grab this opportunity might be outweighed by your fear of leaving your family alone. However, you have to make a decision, and use your discernment to arrive at a conclusion.

This all allows our psychological components to work together toward our consciously set goals rather than being paralyzed by internal conflict. Rather than being a single personality feature, self-discipline is a method of psychological self-regulation.

Face your fears head-on with intellect and actively listen to your rational inner voice, and your emotional voice will have less control over you. Then, you can proceed with fewer roadblocks. This, however, is not to say we don't need our emotional voice, but exercising emotional intelligence is vital.

Additionally, only through consistent exercise—exercise that significantly depends on **self-confidence**—does our self-discipline muscle grow stronger.

When we're stuck in a rut, our self-confidence diminishes and, over time, fades away because we don't use it. Consequently, we don't notice its absence until we need it. Hence, we lack one of the most crucial elements of self-discipline: self-confidence.

To overcome this issue, you must reawaken your sense of self-confidence, which will psychologically strengthen your self-discipline. Always keep in mind that confidence helps discipline. For example, if you're confident that you're prepared for a day's work, it becomes easier to perform your daily tasks efficiently with a definitive mindset.

Therefore, the key to success revolves around your capacity to identify and deal with the aspect of your life that creates resistance, whether you're attempting to maintain a diet, clean your house, or increase your productivity at work.

This is where **willpower** comes in, and in turn we **monitor** our decisions and see how disciplined we are.

So, in essence, the elements of self-discipline makes it easier for us to assess our weak spots, overcome them, and establish ourselves firmly in our long-term goals with confidence. But you must first assess your level of self-control before you can develop discipline.

The beauty of it is that these elements work collaboratively for not just self-discipline, but every area of life too. This is why some of these elements are also the different 'powers' of the mind that drive everyday life and decision making.

Pillar 2:

Mind

◆•————————•●————————•◆

Our minds are more dynamic than we might believe, and capable of reaching the highest heights by simply thinking about something. Whatever we focus on is what gains power, since our brains were built to be flexible, malleable, and susceptible to our influences.

Hence, our experiences serve as the spark for this molding, and everything we think, feel, experience, perceive, and do is gradually modifying the structure of our brains in order to best assist us.

This is why certain things like emotions, willpower, motivation and habits are essential *powers* of the mind, and in turn, shapes the way we perceive things and go about our daily lives.

But what does this have to do with self-discipline? Just about everything, really. In this chapter, we'll discuss the untapped powers of our minds, and how they influence our self-discipline.

Emotions

Although emotions are significant signs that we should pay attention to, allowing them to take control can lead to disciplinary lapses. Consider all the times you've been under a lot of pressure and binge-watched your favorite Netflix series to relax.

Emotional regulation entails becoming aware of your feelings, accepting them without judgment or suppression, and then choosing constructive ways to deal with them. This and emotional intelligence are strongly related.

Let's assume that you're attempting to limit your screen time. For instance, rather than watching another episode of a TV show after learning that your business plan was rejected at work, you can go for a stroll with a friend and let out your frustration. You can acknowledge your emotions without allowing them to derail your goals, even though it's not good to dismiss them. This is called emotional discipline, which is a key component of self-control.

Emotional Discipline

Realizing a seemingly impossible truth—that you can choose how you feel—is one of the finest methods to increase mental vitality.

We all know that feelings are powerful forces. They even sometimes catch up with us. They also have an impact on how we think and act.

We have repeatedly been advised to take heed of our emotions since they are a true reflection of who we are. But emotions can definitely throw us off course. They can cause significant stress and conflict that happen when people disagree.

However, we can gather knowledge about our emotional experience from all of the elements of emotion. In doing this, they also provide opportunities to practice emotional restraint, which is very important when developing self-discipline.

Each of us has a unique set of emotional triggers because we all have had various life experiences. So, there is no one approach to emotional control. Instead, you can create it and modify it to suit your needs.

The main technique entails performing a few straightforward actions each time you experience a major emotional encounter.

Here is a technique you can use to assess and gain emotional discipline:

- **Assess the cause.** Determine the situation or event that causes a particular emotion. What led to the emotions you're feeling during the argument?

- **Assess your body.** Determine where, and how strongly, your emotions are creating physical reactions by scanning your body. Where does anger physically seem like it's affecting you? Consider how pleasant or awful the physical sensation is.

- **Assess your mind.** Determine the beliefs that underlie the feelings as well as the thoughts that go along with them. What thoughts are causing you to feel the way you do? Review the language you're using and the images that are running through your head.

- **Assess your spirit.** Determine which aspects of yourself are most exposed by this emotion (is it your healthy spirit or your anxious ego?).

This will, of course, take practice, and practice makes improvement. Another way you can achieve emotional discipline to better regulate self-discipline is by changing your perspective.

Here are two of the most significant and useful steps that your mind may access:

- **Reframe your mind.** You can transform failures into opportunities for achievement by altering how you view something. When you're facing a challenging emotional circumstance, concentrate on both the opportunities and the risks it presents. For instance, a disagreement offers the opportunity to gain insight into interpersonal dynamics and people's differing perspectives.

- **Mental kung fu.** The goal of kung fu, a Chinese form of self-defense, is to neutralize any assaulting force. Instead of fighting the adversary, you channel their energy toward achieving your objective. With the force of their assault, you knock the opponent to the ground. Emotional disagreements can be resolved using the same strategy. You channel an emotional attack's energy toward finding a solution rather than fighting it. People engage in three behaviors during emotionally charged arguments: they vigorously present their perspectives, criticize our ideas, and attack. Most of the time, we want to fight back, stand up for ourselves, or reject what others say. However, you can avoid and divert the attack's force and use their strength to your advantage. You accept criticism and suggestions that may point to a solution, reframe the attack as one against the issue rather than you, and pose concerns as opposed to making declarations.

Make Negative Emotions Work for You

Each one of us has experienced one of 'those' situations. You know... when a client snaps at you unfairly after weeks of hard work; when your best friend (and coworker) gets abruptly fired; or when your supervisor gives you extra work when you're already overwhelmed.

When faced with difficult circumstances like these in your work life, you can start screaming or run and wallow in self-pity for a while. However, these behaviors at work, or anywhere else, have the potential to dramatically undermine both your productivity and professional reputation. This is why we need self-discipline when faced with negative emotions as well. But in these situations, it can be hard to exercise any level of emotional control.

Even if controlling your emotions may become increasingly difficult in certain situations, it's crucial for you to do so. For example, in the event that management is compelled to make additional layoffs, they may decide to keep individuals who are resilient and perform well under duress. You always have the option to decide how to respond to any given circumstance.

How can you then improve your ability to control your emotions and 'choose' how you respond to challenging circumstances? In this section, we'll examine the most prevalent negative feelings people encounter, their causes, and provide helpful ways to deal with them.

Causes

Numerous things might give rise to negative emotions. Sometimes they are the outcome of particular experiences or circumstances. For instance, you can be furious that your spouse was late for a planned date or disappointed that your favorite football team lost a game.

Negative feelings may also result from:

- **Relationship conflict**. Emotionally unpleasant situations can result from issues in interpersonal relationships. Relationships with friends, relatives, coworkers, or romantic partners may face such difficulties.

- **Unmet needs**. It's normal to feel sad, angry, lonely, envious, and other uncomfortable feelings when your needs—whether they're physical, emotional, social, mental, or spiritual in nature—are not being met.

- **Lack of coping mechanisms**. If you lack the mechanisms to manage daily stress, it can cause a wide range of unpleasant feelings. Poor coping skills frequently lead to the problem getting worse or to the emergence of new issues.

Common Negative Emotions

The following list includes the most prevalent negative feelings encountered in both the workplace and daily life

- frustration/irritation

- worry/nervousness

- anger/aggravation

- dislike

- disappointment/unhappiness

You can utilize the many methods listed below to assist you deal with each of these unpleasant emotions.

Frustration/Irritation

Generally, frustration happens when you feel unable to move forward, confined, or trapped in some other way. It could be brought on by a coworker hindering your chosen task, a boss who is too unorganized to arrive at your appointment on time, or even just a lengthy phone hold.

Whatever the source, it's critical to deal with feelings of frustration as soon as possible since they can quickly turn into more unpleasant emotions, including anger.

Here are a few ideas for reducing frustration:

- One of the greatest things you can do is to take a moment to pause and assess the situation. If you're frustrated, consider why. Put it in writing and be specific. Then consider one advantage of your current circumstance. For instance, you could use the extra time to prepare if your boss is late for the meeting. Or you could take a moment to unwind.

- Find a good side to the situation. Thinking about a positive point of your circumstances will help you see things differently. This minor shift in perspective can lift your spirits. When other people are the source of your annoyance, they are probably not doing it on purpose. And if there's something bothering you, it's most definitely nothing personal! Don't be angry; simply continue.

- When was the last time you were irritated? When you were last upset over something, it most likely resolved itself after some time, right? It's likely that your displeasure or annoyance didn't help much to resolve the issue back then, and it follows that it won't help you today either.

Worry/Nervousness

It's understandable that many people are concerned about their careers, goals and life. However, if you let it, this fear may quickly spiral out of control and negatively affect not only your mental wellbeing but also your productivity and willingness to take chances.

Try these strategies to stop worrying:

- Avoid being surrounded by anxiety and worry. For instance, if coworkers are chatting about layoffs in the break room, resist the urge to join them in their fear. Nobody benefits when they worry since worrying often results in more worrying.

- Try deep breathing techniques to help you breathe more slowly and lower your heart rate. Take a five-second deep breath in, followed by a five-second deep breath out. Only pay attention to your breathing. Repeat this five times minimum.

- Concentrate on ways to make things better. You won't likely be able to keep your job, start a new project, launch a business plan or take control of your diet if, out of fear of failing, you sit there and worry. Instead, why not come up with creative strategies to encourage success?

- Write your problems down in a "worry log." If you notice that your issues are circling in your head, write them down and then set aside a time to address them. Put these concerns to rest until then since you know you'll take care of them. Conduct a thorough risk analysis of these circumstances when it comes to the time you've allotted, and then take the appropriate steps to reduce any risks.

Your confidence can suffer if you're anxious and worried about any-thing . Don't let your worries prevent you from being assertive in the right way either. Remember, self-discipline walks hand in hand with self-confidence.

Anger/Aggravation

Perhaps the most damaging emotion that people encounter is out-of-control fury. Additionally, it's the emotion that the majority of us have trouble managing. The best way to control anger is through practicing self-control, which is also a key component of self-discipline.

To manage your anger, consider the following ideas:

- Keep an eye out for early indications of anger. You alone are the one who can spot the warning signals of rage developing. Early control of your anger is essential. Keep in mind that you have a choice in how you respond to events. Just because becoming upset is your initial impulse, doesn't mean that it's the best course of action.

- Pause whatever you're doing if you find yourself getting upset, close your eyes, and perform the deep breathing exercise we previously discussed. This cuts off your angry thoughts and helps you get back on the right track.

- Imagine yourself in a furious state. You can gain some perspective on the circumstance if you picture how you might appear and act in a furious state. Consider how you would appear if you were about to yell at a coworker. Is your face rosy? Do you have your arms raised? Would you desire to work with anyone like that? Most likely not.

Dislike

At work most of all, we've all had to collaborate with people we don't like. However, it's imperative to maintain professionalism at all times.

Here are some suggestions for dealing with those you dislike:

- Be respectful. It's time to put your pride and ego aside if you have to work with somebody you don't get along with. Like you would with anyone else, be courteous and respectful to the person. You shouldn't act in an unprofessional manner simply because the other person does.

- Be assertive. If the other person is being impolite and disrespectful, strongly state that you'll not tolerate such behavior, and then quietly leave the situation. Always lead by example.

Disappointment/Unhappiness

It might be challenging to deal with disappointment or discontent. Of all the emotions you could experience, these feelings are the most likely to affect your productivity. After a significant setback, your energy will likely be low, you might be hesitant to take a risk again, and all of these things could prevent you from accomplishing your goals.

You can take the following proactive measures to deal with disappointment and unhappiness:

- Examine your mentality. Recognize for a minute that not everything will go your way. If it did, wouldn't life be a straight route without ups and downs, hills and valleys? These hills and valleys are what frequently add interest to life.

- Reconsider your aim. Just because you were unhappy that you didn't achieve a goal doesn't mean that it's now impossible to achieve. Maintain the objective but make a minor adjustment, like delaying the deadline.

- Keep a thought journal and list the specific reasons why you're unhappy in writing. Is it a colleague? Do you have a lot on your plate? Once the issue has been located, begin formulating solutions or workarounds. Always keep in mind that you have the ability to change your circumstances.

- Put a smile on your face. Although it may sound unusual, smiling can frequently make you feel cheerful. It's weird, but it's a part of who we are as humans. So give it a try; you might be surprised!

Unhealthy Ways of Coping

Unhelpful or even harmful coping mechanisms are unfortunately frequently used to deal with bad emotions. Although they could offer short-term respite, these usually lead to long-term problems getting worse.

Ignoring Feelings

The healthiest approach to dealing with emotions is to not ignore them. In general, it doesn't make feelings go away, but it can make them come out differently; for example, pausing for a moment, realizing that you're angry, and taking a few deep breaths might prevent you from yelling at your child.

Negative feelings are a warning that your current course of action is lacking. As a result, when you neglect them, you're unable to change and continue to feel bad.

Pondering Emotions

Rumination entails fixating on unpleasant emotions like resentment and anger. Detrimental emotions are amplified, but there are also negative effects on one's health. Therefore, it's crucial to pay attention to your emotions before expressing them.

Avoidance or Withdrawal

You may find yourself attempting to avoid uncomfortable situations so that you won't have to feel those terrible feelings. For instance, you might take precautions to avoid your anxiety triggers if they are a specific person or circumstance. The issue is that avoidance as a coping mechanism, ultimately makes bad emotions worse.

Risky or Destructive Behaviors

The emotions you're experiencing can affect both your physical and emotional health, if you don't deal with them. This is especially true if you adopt dangerous activities to deal with upsetting emotions, such substance abuse or self-harm.

Emotions affect everyone, and it's more crucial than ever to understand how to deal with negative feelings when they arise. After all, unfavorable feelings can spread, and nobody wants to be with someone who makes the group uncomfortable.

Recognize the roots of your bad emotions and the predominant sentiments you experience. Start implementing your plan to break the pattern, as soon as those emotions start to surface. In essence, with practice, this all increases your level of restraint and develops self-discipline.

Managing Motivation

No matter how disciplined you are, if you're putting effort into something you don't really care about, it won't matter. If you notice that you're consistently engaging in activities that are in conflict with your goal, consider if you genuinely want that long-term target . Asking yourself why you desire that long-term objective is crucial. The truth may dawn on you that you don't.

For example, if you have a goal of buying a new car in the next two years. You'll have to cut back on spending and start saving to get this car. But what if you find that you don't really have the enthusiasm to do this? Does it mean you have no self-discipline? Not necessarily.

Consider re-evaluating your long-term objective of getting a new car rather than criticizing yourself for not having "enough self-discipline." You might discover that it's not at all what you wanted. Perhaps you felt pushed into it because all your friends own expensive cars and society tells you that that's what's respectable. But maybe you love your old car, and your motivation might be to service it, not get rid of or replace it.

You might discover that you weren't setting the right goals in the first place and that you don't actually have an issue with self-discipline.

You'll also remain motivated to pick the long-term benefit over the temporary pleasure, if you choose goals that truly mean and matter to you. This, in its own capacity, is truly a key component of self-discipline.

So What Exactly Is Motivation?

Motivation can be summed up as a willingness to complete an action. When working on something, it's a terrific asset to have because it drives you to finish the project. For instance, wanting to lose weight might be a big incentive to get up early and go for a run. The same thing can happen to your performance when your supervisor is upset or when a deadline is looming.

Most of the time, people struggle to start. For instance, they put off starting something until they absolutely must. This is why the world is changed through motivation. Starting a task becomes a lot easier when you're motivated and excited to finish it. Even better, you work more quickly and efficiently when you're enthusiastic about the project. For this reason, people believe that motivation is the most crucial element in habit formation. Yes, it can help us achieve previously unimaginable goals, but how long will it last?

The issue with motivation is that it wanes earlier than you anticipate. You must be on the lookout for motivation killers.

Let's say you made the decision to work out for a month. In the first week of a new habit, you feel motivated and as though nothing could stop you from achieving your objective. However, one day your manager calls and criticizes you for failing to complete the last project well. You naturally start to feel frustrated and anxious. But this unpleasant surprise does more than just hurt your professional prospects. You'll almost certainly miss a workout and mess up your routine when you're irritated. This, and other frequent errors, might make it simple for a new habit to fail.

The fact is that developing habits requires both motivation and self-discipline. If you understand how to apply them properly, they actually go together flawlessly. For instance, motivation can act as a catalyst at the beginning, while self-discipline is excellent for maintaining focus.

Making self-discipline practical and maintaining that focus are the two primary challenges that many people encounter. If you're having a similar problem, the following advice will be helpful to you:

- Only think of motivation as the start of a habit. Motivation won't keep you focused for very long, as was already mentioned. Don't assume that motivation will still affect you after a month.

- Choose what is best for you. Set clear priorities and identify your needs. You won't adopt the required mindset if you don't know what is best for you.

- Make your choice right away. Before beginning, decide on all the actions required to attain your goal.

- Connect inspiration to good things. Self-discipline is the light that illuminates the path to the goal, while motivation is the fuel. It's better to keep in mind that the outcome ultimately benefits your life in some way.

How To Get Motivated

You already understand what motivation entails and how it functions. Now is the time to put your knowledge into practice. You may replace temptations and procrastination with motivation and productivity by taking the four concrete steps listed below.

Write Down Goals and Keep Them Visible

Writing down your goals causes a specific brain region to become active, which in some way makes you more responsible. We psychologically adjust ourselves to stay on course as soon as we put down our goals. Why keep it visible? If you waver, it will act as a reminder as to why you began.

Track Development and Recognize The Smallest Successes

Recognizing that you're already midway to your goals is one of the few things that could motivate you more. Two significant things occur when you track your development. First, you become aware of your progress from the beginning. It also provides you a reason to reward yourself. Track development and recognize accomplishments.

Surround Yourself with Achievers and Highly Motivated People

Taking this action might be one of the most crucial of all. If, for example, everyone in your family eats pizza almost every night, it becomes practically impossible to keep a healthy diet.

Ensure that at least half of the individuals in your immediate circle are inspired and motivated. We all experience ups and downs, and when you're experiencing a down period, you'll need a driven companion by your side to encourage you to go on.

Establish Due Dates and Smaller Deadlines

Commitments have deadlines. Our brain receives cues from commitments to keep working hard, no matter what. Isn't that the main goal of motivation? Being organized and avoiding distractions are two other benefits of deadlines. You owe it to yourself to finish your smaller chores by setting micro-deadlines. Make sure each sub-goal in your blueprint has a set of micro-deadlines. Say, for example, you have a presentation due in 30 days, but you need a few things at the bookstore to complete it. Give yourself a deadline to go shopping for your supplies in order to get your presentation done on time.

You can use motivation to help you reach your goals, set you off to a clean start, and keep you going in the right direction until you achieve your aspirations. Most importantly, it will help you stay focused on your goals, create effective self-discipline, and even make some healthy habits.

Wielding Willpower

The psychology field has long believed that willpower is a limited resource. This is in part due to the self-regulation hypothesis developed by social psychologist Roy Baumeister, the idea of ego depletion, and the numerous studies that have supported both (Fingerprint for Success, n.d).

Ego depletion basically says that the more willpower you exert, the less of it you actually have. You spend the week being "good" about your nutrition and avoiding carbs and sugar, so by the time the weekend arrives, you binge on all the treats you could get your hands on. Maybe you've had similar experiences.

But recent studies have questioned the validity of ego depletion. Prior research on ego depletion had been compromised by publication bias (Fingerprint for Success, n.d).

Willpower, according to more modern thinking, is a resource that never runs out. Willpower is more related to mindset: If you believe your willpower is excludable, you'll lose momentum. However, if you think you have enough willpower, you'll keep going.

What function, then, should willpower serve in your pursuit of self-discipline? According to research, the most effective way to attain one's aim is to avoid temptations rather than resist them (Fingerprint for Success, n.d).

Instead of attempting to muster your willpower, which already seems unpredictable, arrange your life so that you're not dependent on it.

And here's how.

Get Rid of Temptations

Those who are particularly disciplined don't possess more willpower than others; rather, they are able to avoid using it. Indeed, individuals who are good at self-control seem to plan their lives in a way to prevent needing to make a self-control choice in the first place.

Additionally, planning your life is a talent. People who engage in the same activity, such as jogging or meditation, at the same time every day, have an easier time reaching their goals. This is because the pattern makes it simpler rather than because of their willpower.

Do you want to consume less junk food? Avoid keeping soda, candy bars, and chips around the house. Want to spend less time on your devices? Place your phone in a drawer and keep it there all day. Want to start out for a run each morning? Keep your jogging shoes close by and your alarm across the room.

In other words, make it simple for yourself to make the proper decisions, if you want to improve your ability to forgo rapid satisfaction in a world filled with temptations. This brings us to the second trait of self-disciplined individuals: healthy habits.

Develop Positive Habits

As we discussed earlier, our brains become so accustomed to some habits that we don't even have to think about them. This lack of choice is good, since it indicates that habitual behavior rather than willpower is at play.

Forming a habit involves four steps:

- There's a **cue** that sets off the habit.

- There's a **desire** to change your state or satisfy the feeling.

- There's a **response** to the urge or desire.

- Your behavior will yield **rewards**, that is, the outcome of the actions.

With this process in mind, it's clear how undesirable habits develop. For example, if you want to lay back on your soda intake for health reasons, this is what happens:

- You're thirsty after eating a granola bar, and this is the **cue**.

- You crave a soda to quench this thirst which is the **desire**.

- Your **response** is to go to the canteen and get one from the fridge.

- The soda quenches your thirst, being the **reward**.

However, the same procedure also applies to healthy habits. In the case above, you may substitute something else for soda rather than declare that you wish to stop drinking soda, which is a deeply rooted habit. For instance, a freshly squeezed box of orange juice can be used in place of soda to quench your thirst.

So, discipline need not solely consist of control and constraint. You don't have to give up your desire for a refreshing drink and a healthier lifestyle. Easily substitute it with an item that supports your long-term objectives of better nutrition.

By carrying out these actions, positive habits develop and self-discipline becomes second nature.

Rash Behavior and Self-Control

Self-control is the ability to override your ideas and feelings, allowing you to adaptively change conduct from one situation to the next. To prevent bad behaviors, promote favorable ones, and accomplish long-term goals, you must be able to manage and modify your reactions.

Common objectives like regular exercise, a healthy diet, increased productivity, kicking bad habits, and financial savings are just a few excellent desires that typically demand self-control to accomplish.

Improving Self-Control

Self-control may have its limits, but psychologists have discovered that it may be increased through the use of specific techniques.

Refuse Temptation

Achieving the most out of your potential self-control is possible by resisting temptation. In this way, you can prevent "using up" your limited self-control before it's truly necessary.

Finding a healthy diversion is one approach to resist temptation, regardless of whether the urge is to consume food, alcohol, spend money, or engage in other undesirable behaviors or bad habits.

Concentrate on One Task at a Time

A common ineffective strategy is to set a lot of objectives at once. Self-control can be affected in other areas when your willpower is depleted in one. It's advisable to select a single objective and concentrate all of your efforts on it.

You won't have to exert as much energy maintaining your goal-achieving actions, once you've made them habits. Then you can use your assets to work toward other objectives.

Keep the Consequences in Mind

Lack of self-control can have negative impacts on your self-esteem, education, profession, finances, relationships, and general health and well-being. Just as it can hinder you from achieving your goals and worsen your mental and physical health. You can stay motivated as you attempt to improve your self-control by reminding yourself of these repercussions.

Plan in Advance

Think about events that might make you lose your determination. What steps will you take if you're tempted, in order to resist giving up? Planning ahead has been shown to increase willpower even in circumstances where people have felt the impacts of self-esteem depletion (Cherry, 2022).

Learn to Exercise Self-Control

While engaging in habits that test your self-control on a regular basis will help you build willpower over time, they may temporarily drain your control. Consider self-control to be a muscle. While intense exercise may temporarily wear a muscle out, with continued use, the muscle will get stronger.

Meditate

You can build up your capacity for self-control by practicing meditation. Being more self-aware will help you resist temptation more effectively. This method can also teach you to pause your thoughts, which can teach you to regulate gut feelings that might otherwise interfere with your self-control.

Self-control is something you can develop with experience and effort. You may better control your behavior by avoiding temptations, developing a strategy, concentrating on specific objectives, and being aware of the repercussions of your choices.

Pillar 3:

Body

* * *

Following a healthy food and exercise regimen wouldn't be difficult in a flawless, predictable, and stress-free world. But since that isn't how things actually work, you should prepare for setbacks if you want to maintain your self-discipline and develop good habits. It can be beneficial to take some time each day to unwind your body and mind, by doing some meditation and obtaining enough sleep.

Keep nutritious snacks close at hand; when food cravings for items not on your diet plan strike, take a healthy snack to ward off hunger and aid in satisfying the craving. Planning quick, 10-minute bursts of exercise, such as taking the stairs at work or jogging, might help you resist the need to snack while breaking down your fitness goals into manageable pieces. Setting realistic short- and long-term goals is important for retaining self-discipline. Because of hectic work and family schedules, exercising every day a week might not be feasible. A more realistic objective is to work out five days each week.

Benchmarks for your long-term objectives should be established by short-term objectives. If you want to lose weight, for instance, set a six-month goal but divide it up into smaller chunks, like losing a pound every two weeks. By achieving these mini-milestones, you can maintain your motivation, which is a factor in keeping your self-discipline. In the end, you're rewarded with healthy, established habits too.

Don't worry about instances when you cave in to temptation if you want to maintain good self-discipline. If you ate dessert at dinner one night or choose to stay in bed an additional 30 minutes rather than waking up to work out, be kind to yourself and stop beating yourself up over it.

Instead, make the most of these distractions to help you refocus by reviewing your long- and short-term goals again and, if required, making minor adjustments to make them more attainable. Renew your motivation; after a brief rest, it's time to get back to work. Anxiety from worrying about times when you didn't stick to your food, sleep and exercise regimen can prevent you from being as disciplined as you were before the slip-up.

Consider the circumstances that may have led to the lack of self-discipline. After all, your good self-discipline and healthy habits didn't just happen overnight.

So with that said, this chapter will focus on how taking care of your body influences self-discipline and habit building.

The Effects of Nutrition on Self-Discipline

Self-control really exists! It also works if you take the necessary steps to give your self-discipline the push it needs.

Feeding your brain the glucose it requires for energy is among the things you can do to boost your confidence, resilience, and self-discipline.

Your brain depends on glucose, as well as water and other nutrients, to survive. Steak alone won't keep your brain alive. It just plainly won't work. So you must start ingesting glucose if you want to improve your self-discipline.

The brain consumes about 20% of our daily calories although making up only 2% of our total weight (Lindley, 2016). It's a fussy eater and needs a steady supply of glucose, which is mostly derived from previously consumed carbs; fruits, vegetables, grains etc. The brain won't use other chemicals as fuel unless there is a severe lack of food or other resources.

According to Leigh Gibson of Roehampton University in England, brain regions controlling important functions are more resilient to declining glucose levels than regions of the brain, such the frontal cortex, that have developed more recently (Lindley, 2016). According to Gibson, disturbed thinking, rather than a change in breathing rhythm, is the indication of low blood sugar (Lindley, 2016).

Therefore, following a low-carb diet is essentially asking for your self-discipline to collapse. Since your executive decisions are produced in the frontal cortex, which acts like the CEO of the brain. You're more prone to make bad choices and develop bad habits if you avoid high-quality carbs. We don't really want any additional roadblocks in our way when we're attempting to accomplish our aims.

So, what types of carbohydrates—or, as they were formerly known, starches—benefit the brain?

- **Sweet potatoes:** Sweet potatoes release sugar gradually. These delicious vegetables slowly release glucose into your bloodstream when you eat them. That's advantageous because what we want is good glucose for the brain over a prolonged length of time. This can be your go-to snack when you're training your brain. Your energy levels, as well as mental function, may remain high all day long.

- **Legumes/Lentils:** In theory, you might classify these as beans, but in some nations, lentils are distinguished from other legumes. Lentils can also be cooked, or purchased in a can, (watch the salt content!) and added to a salad or soup. Like beans, they are filling and give you the glucose you need to maintain your self-discipline.

- **Beans:** Beans are suitable here; any kind will do. Hummus will also work, but beware of some shop brands' high fat content. You may set the goal of consuming one cup of beans every day. Both your brain and your weight will benefit greatly from it. Beans give you the fuel you need to be focused and alert while also filling you up.

- **Whole Grains:** Whole grains can be found in processed foods like bread, pasta, and other baked goods. The phrase "WHOLE Grain" is the key component. Beware of organic products that aren't whole grain or products that claim to be whole grain but only feature it as the last ingredient on the label.

Adding these foods to your diet will feed your brain and help you overcome cravings, negative habits, and self-destructive behavior.

What Nutrients Are Needed for Self-Discipline?

We spoke about some foods you may consume on a regular basis to help develop self-discipline to create better habits. But what nutrients does the brain really require to do this apart from carbohydrates and good glucose?

As we know, a nutritious, well-balanced diet can be beneficial for both physical and mental health. A study also highlighted the significance of nutrients in goals, identity, mood improvement, and motivation, all of which might boost your level of self-discipline (McCarthy et al.,

2017). While it might not seem to have a big impact right away, nutrition does play a part in how you manage your emotions over time, which has a big impact on your productivity, thinking process and inevitably, habits.

Omega-3s

You should obtain omega-3 fatty acids from the foods you eat since they are necessary for building cell wall structure and for an overall healthy body. Omega-3 fatty acids can support cognitive functions and prevent brain-aging. Salmon and sardines are two fatty fish that are particularly rich in these minerals. Walnuts and flaxseeds, however, also contain significant amounts of omega-3s.

Vitamin B

B vitamins are also essential for healthy cognitive and other brain functions. The B vitamins you should aim to have in your diet for mindset, cognition, and motivation are thiamin (B1), riboflavin (B2), niacin (B3), pantothenic acid (B5), pyridoxine (B6), biotin (B7), folate (B9), and cobalamin (B12) (Bejelly, 2021). Furthermore, because B vitamins provide you energy and unleash the brain's potential, they can help you make the best use of your creative mind and the motivation you already possess. What better way to boost habit building?

Magnesium

Magnesium may be helpful in reducing stress, which can occasionally hinder our drive and self-discipline since we are more susceptible to 'let it be' when we are under duress. Insufficient sleep can also be a factor, but magnesium-rich foods like dark chocolate, fruits, and nuts can help you develop and maintain sound sleep patterns.

Choline

Because it indirectly influences neurotransmitters, choline—which is present in foods including fish, meat, poultry, almonds, whole grains, fruits, and vegetables—is crucial for mood and cognitive function. Choline's ability to reduce brain fog may help maintain a clear mind to make healthy decisions throughout the day, as well as maintain focus until the completion of a task.

Vitamin K

Another crucial component for vision, inspiration, and productivity is vitamin K. You can get a good amount of vitamin K from broccoli and dark leafy greens, which can maintain your brain health and avoid weariness, which in turn, can lower your levels of discipline.

Antioxidants

Finally, antioxidants help reduce oxidative stress, which in some cases might heighten anxiety and despair and affect levels of motivation and self-awareness. By lowering inflammation and safeguarding brain cells, antioxidants also support brain health.

Food Tips for Developing and Maintaining Self-Discipline

If you believe that your food is having a negative impact on your energy, productivity, mindset, and discipline, there are a few things to keep in mind.

Avoid Sugar

The majority of individuals desire to remain purposeful or motivated during the workday, yet when stress strikes, they reach for a candy bar or a caffeinated beverage. In the long run, as the sugary high wears off and you crash, you quickly realize that this is not the ideal solution and can affect your self-discipline. You may have brain fog and exhaustion as a result of this come-down, making it much more difficult to recall your earlier-in-the-day goals and remain level-headed. Not to mention that this is a bad habit in the making.

Follow a Balanced Diet

Eating a healthy, balanced diet guarantees that you are getting the nutrition you need for optimal brain performance. This can assist you in maintaining an optimistic outlook, which can support your desire for increased concentration and productivity. Make an effort to include fruits, veggies, and nuts in your daily diet.

Prepare/Plan Your Lunch the Previous Evening

When stress strikes, convenience takes precedence over nutritional value. When this occurs, the sugar crash is more likely to occur just as you require an energy boost. You can be sure that there will be a better selection available if you arrange your meals the night before. You can eat everything you require to be attentive and focused.

Snack More Often During the Day

No, I'm not suggesting you eat more desserts. To get you to your next meal, try reaching for some fruit or nuts. Your glucose levels will be better balanced as a result, preventing a crash. Snacks during the day will keep you alert and able to complete even the most complicated tasks.

Avoid Addictions

Although this is less of 'food' and more of substances, it's crucial that you avoid any addictions that improve your physical and mental health if you want to develop self-discipline. This is crucial since building oneself requires being awake, which is impossible if you're addicted to various intoxicants.

The two addictions that are most prevalent nowadays are drinking and smoking. It's essential to overcome these two addictions as soon as possible because they can impair the functioning of practically all of the body's organs. It would be beneficial if you could find some effective substitutes to help you quit smoking and drinking over time.

The use of nicotine replacement therapy, which delivers nicotine to the body in tiny amounts, can be a great way to stop smoking. While beverages like lemonade and iced tea can be suitable replacements for alcohol.

Try these suggestions for a change if you wish to boost your cognitive function, which affects your self-discipline. When you modify your diet, you'll notice a difference in your energy level and quality of focus. Change some basic dietary habits to feel better and accomplish more!

The Effects of Physical Activity on Self-Discipline

If you aren't physically healthy, you may inadvertently be attracting many illnesses. Even if you believe that in today's automated world you don't need to exercise your body, you still need to keep it in top shape. You never know what type of complication you might face in the next instant of your life. Additionally, exercising is one of the best ways to improve self-discipline and prepare yourself for all of your daily tasks.

Unfortunately, a lot of people never really benefit from exercise since they set unattainable training goals and can't maintain consistency. When creating an exercise schedule, keep in mind that reliability is considerably more crucial than regularity. It makes no difference whether you begin by lifting weights or by taking a walk. If you're consistent, you'll strengthen your self-discipline and develop both physical and mental strength! The advantages don't stop there, either. According to a Macquarie University in Sydney study, some other benefits of exercising on self-discipline include (Robertson, 2014):

- less procrastination

- feeling more in charge of emotions

- a reduction in cigarette, alcohol, and caffeine consumption

- better control over finances

- healthier eating

- less screen time

- more productivity

- less impulsive purchases

These actions simply can come about organically as a result of a regular workout!

The trick is that exercise doesn't necessarily have to influence your self-discipline. Most of the time, it's the fact that you're *training* your mind to set apart this time from the day to exercise, that builds your discipline to do so. Eventually, your self-discipline will become more rounded to accommodate your other tasks. Hence, you'll notice you have no time to procrastinate, or you realize you're more willing to control what you eat.

Of course, there are some neurological benefits as well, where exercise directly influences the health of your brain. In all, you build your self-discipline, and of course, build good habits too.

How Much Exercise Do You Need?

Let's pause quickly before you create a strategy to transition from not working out at all to exercising every day. It's critical to keep in mind that you don't have to visit the gym everyday; perhaps just once each week for the entire month.

It's obvious that you don't have to start your fitness regimen at zero and work your way up to a hundred immediately. Make a regular, manageable plan in order to start enjoying all of the advantages mentioned above. It doesn't matter if you can workout once a week or four times a week. You only need to create a plan that you won't abandon, in order to reap the rewards.

What Type of Exercise Should You Do?

What kind of "physical activity" should you be engaging in is likely the next question on many people's minds.

But the real question is, what kind of workout are you willing to participate in?

The kind of exercise you pick may have a variety of physical advantages, but the brain doesn't really care. If you jog or do pull-ups, you'll essentially experience identical self-discipline advantages. You'll experience the benefits of exercise on your self-discipline as long as you're not lying down, sitting, or remaining still. Simply taking a walk has great advantages for your health and mind. As a result, if you're just starting out, avoid creating a demanding and daunting training schedule. Just begin simply and continue.

Overcoming Exercising Roadblocks

Getting started is still easier said than done, even when you understand that exercise could increase discipline and give birth to a new healthy habit. Exercise-related difficulties are quite real, especially if you're also suffering with a mental health illness or other life troubles.

Here are some typical obstacles and solutions.

Feeling Tired

It seems like exercising can only make you feel worse when you're exhausted, unhappy, or under stress. But the fact remains that exercise is a potent energizer. According to studies, regular exercise greatly lowers fatigue and increases energy levels (Robinson et al., 2021). If you're truly tired, make a 5-minute commitment to go for a short walk. Once you get moving, you'll probably have more energy and be able to move easier.

Feeling Unprepared

You can find easy ways to move more if you've never worked out before. Start slowly by walking or dancing for a few minutes a day to get your body moving.

Feeling Self-Conscious

Do you ever find fault with yourself? It's time to try looking at your discipline to exercise from a different angle. Many people are in the same situation as you are. Even small fitness goals can help you be more self-disciplined and give you more confidence.

Being In Pain

Talk to your doctor about safe ways to exercise if you have a serious weight problem, arthritis, or any injury or illness that makes it hard for you to move around. You shouldn't ignore pain. Instead, when you can, you should do something about it. If it helps, divide the time you spend working out into shorter, more frequent chunks. To ease joint or muscle pain, you can also try exercising in water.

Being Overburdened

When you're stressed, the idea of adding another commitment to your already busy day can seem scary. In this case, it might not seem like a good idea to work out. Even if you have a full schedule, you might be able to find time for short workouts when you start to see it as important for your mental health. This is what self-discipline is all about.

How To Get Started

Many people find it challenging enough to obtain the motivation to exercise, even when circumstances are perfect. However, it can seem twice as difficult if you're experiencing stress, or trying to break habits that seem impossible. But once you get started, you can remain consistent if you hold onto your goals. So, let's see how to actually get started.

Start Small

Setting excessive goals like finishing a marathon or exercising for an hour every morning, can just make you feel more defeated if you don't achieve them. That is, if you're just starting out with your exercise regime. Set realistic objectives first, for example, a ten minute walk, then progress from there.

Plan Your Workouts When You're Most Energetic

Perhaps you feel the most energized immediately before you leave for work in the morning, or maybe it's after lunch, just before the afternoon slump hits. Maybe you get more out of your workouts if you extend them on the weekends. When you start moving your body, you'll release endorphins that boost your mood and give you the energy to do more. You might go for a longer walk, start jogging, or ride a bike instead of just walking.

Get Relaxed

Go somewhere you feel relaxed or energized, and dress casually. It could be your favorite city park, a quiet corner of your home, or a scenic drive.

Reward Yourself

Part of the incentive is the sense of achievement you'll get from working out, but an excellent method to increase motivation and develop discipline, is to guarantee yourself a particular reward for exercising. Consider rewarding yourself with a soothing soak in the tub, a refreshing smoothie, or even just one more episode of your favorite show after a tough workout.

Concentrate on Things You Like To Do

It doesn't matter what you do, as long as you move. This could include riding a bike to the grocery store, playing Frisbee with a dog or friends, or walking laps through a mall window-shopping. Try a few different activities if you've never worked out before, or are unsure of what you might enjoy. These activities not only encourage increased activity but also provide a feeling of purpose and achievement.

To reap the various advantages of exercise, you don't need to drag yourself through tiresome, protracted workouts or spend hours in the gym. These suggestions can help you discover activities you enjoy so that you can begin to feel better, build good habits, and enjoy life more.

Extra Tip: Cold showers are one of the best techniques to develop self-discipline and can significantly improve your life. Additionally, it has been a time-tested method used by soldiers and others interested in meditation and spirituality to develop emotional fortitude and willpower.

If you think it will be difficult for you to take cold showers every day, try it once a week and then gradually increase the frequency. The only way to harden your mind is to do it frequently, regardless of how you feel about doing it.

The Effects of Sleep on Self-Discipline

Look at the last time you didn't receive adequate sleep for a moment. The next day, how did you feel? Tired? Irritable? Stressed? These are only a few of the issues that frequently arise after a bad night of sleep, but one very significant side effect is a diminished capacity for self-discipline. In other words, even when we know we should, it's more difficult to restrain our urges and instincts when we are sleep-deprived.

What kinds of urges and impulses are difficult to control? Classic demonstrations of self-discipline include refraining from indulging in a tub of ice cream when on a diet, stopping yourself from spending excessively on a watch you don't need, and keeping your lips sealed when an unpleasant employer yells at you. In other words, exercising self-discipline is resisting our urges when we know they won't benefit us in the long run.

Additionally, lacking sleep makes it more difficult to maintain self-discipline. People are more prone to disrespect others, steal pens and paper, and stop working out early after a night of bad or insufficient sleep.

Therefore, getting 7-8 hours of sleep is crucial for maintaining mental clarity during the day and enhancing your overall quality of life.

Avoid using electronics like laptops and smartphones two hours before going to bed if you want to obtain a good night's sleep. This is because the "blue light" that these devices create interferes with our ability to fall asleep and keeps us up all night. Additionally, endeavor to go to bed at the same time each night so that your body can develop a sleep-inducing internal clock. This also is a good sleeping habit.

Below are some additional tips for getting enough sleep.

Tips for Getting More Sleep

There are several factors that can prevent you from getting a good night's sleep, such as illness, family responsibilities, and work-related stress. It's understandable that regular sleep patterns can be difficult to follow at times.

There may be factors beyond your control that prevent you from getting enough rest. However, it's possible to improve your sleeping conditions by establishing routines and habits. Let's get started with some basic pointers.

Pay Attention to Your Diet

Avoid both overeating and going to bed hungry. In particular, you should always avoid eating a large, heavy meal right before bed. Your discomfort could prevent you from falling asleep.

Additionally, moderate your intake of alcoholic beverages, caffeinated beverages, and nicotine. Energy from nicotine and caffeine can last for hours and make it difficult to fall asleep. Even though alcohol makes you feel sleepy initially, it can disrupt your sleep later on.

Restricting Daytime Naps

Taking a nap for long periods of time during the day can disrupt your sleep at night. Make sure to limit naps to no more than an hour in length, and afternoon naps should be avoided altogether.

However, if you work evenings, you might want to catch some Zs in the afternoon before heading in.

Engage in Physical Activity on a Daily Basis

If you exercise regularly, it can help you achieve better sleeping habits. However, try not to get in a workout right before night-time. Getting some fresh air and sunshine every day may help, too.

Follow a Sleep Schedule

Don't sleep more than eight hours a night. A healthy adult requires at least seven hours of sleep every night. Most of the time, eight hours in bed is all you need to get a good night's sleep.

Every day, even on the weekends, go to bed and wake up at the same time. By being consistent, you can help your body's sleep-wake cycle, and also make yourself more self-disciplined.

If you lie down and try to sleep for 20 minutes and still can't, get out of bed and do something relaxing. Read a novel or play some music that calms you down. When you're tired, go to bed again. If you have trouble falling asleep, try going to bed at least 15 minutes before your "bedtime" to make up for any time you might lose during your sleep hours. Also, use an alarm clock to wake yourself up.

Establish a Peaceful Environment

Make sure your room is nice and cool, quiet, and dark. Exposure to light in the evening could make it more difficult to fall asleep. Try not to stare at screens that emit light right before bed. Consider using earplugs, a fan, room-darkening drapes, or other objects to create an atmosphere that suits your needs.

Taking part in relaxing activities, including taking a bath or doing relaxation exercises, may also help you fall asleep more easily.

Minimize Anxiety

Try to relax and let go of whatever problems you have right before bed. Put your thoughts on paper and set them away for the time being. Get down to basics like planning, prioritizing, and delegating tasks. It helps if you try to reduce your stress levels before bed.. Moreover, meditating can help you reduce anxious feelings.

Knowing When to Contact Your Doctor

Having trouble falling asleep is a common problem that affects everyone. However, make sure to see a doctor if you have chronic sleep problems. Finding and treating the cause of your sleep problems may help you get the restful nights you need.

As humans, we know we need sleep. Just like food and physical activity, it affects our minds and our ability to grasp self-discipline. Getting adequate sleep is essential for not only our health, but to build good habits, resist impulsive actions and maintain overall good self-discipline.

Pillar 4:

Relationships

As we all know, we humans are all social beings. The people around us affect us, as we affect them. Even without realizing it, we might find ourselves adopting habits or behaviors from others, and they might adopt habits from us as well.

Have you ever spent time around someone who says a particular word or phrase a lot, and in a few weeks you notice yourself saying that word or phrase in a situation that warrants it?

The same can be for habits, which is why we should surround ourselves with highly motivated, effective individuals. Likewise, we should also aim to be such people, especially if we have younger people depending on us to be an example.

In this chapter, we will talk about the roles of interpersonal relationships on our habits and behaviors.

The Role of Family and Friends in Shaping Your Habits

The communities and groups that we interact with are one way that our social environment affects our habits.

Both in major and minor ways, this is true. Our conduct can be influenced by large groups, like governments, religions organizations, and businesses. Additionally, small groups, like the area in which you reside, or the charity you support might have an impact on your behavior.

Our sense of belonging is the most important aspect of any of these communities. We want to emulate the behaviors of the group we wish to be a part of. So, we unconsciously adopt the habits of people around us. For example:

- You might begin gardening or landscaping your yard if you relocate to a new community where your neighbors take great care of their lawns.

- If you start attending CrossFit classes where all of your other participants follow a Keto diet, you might decide to do the same.

- You may start volunteering your time if you attend a church or mosque that emphasizes community service.

Our expectations of what is "normal" are shaped by our culture. Be with people who practice the habits you wish to adopt for yourself. Together, you will succeed.

But what about family and friends? What about those closest to you in blood or relation? Do they have an impact on your habits as well as groups and community? Most definitely. Maybe even more so than random external groups!

When you observe family and friends practicing new behaviors every day, they seem doable. If you grew up with siblings who loved to read, you're more likely to think of reading as a habit. You're more likely to start recycling if you're surrounded by people in your household who recycle.

This is why it's so important to keep friends with like-minded achievements after you accomplish a goal, in order to keep your habits in place. The long-term sustainability of habits and the establishment of new identities depend on friendships and family.

Paying it Forward—How Your Actions Affect Others

Your habits and actions can influence those around you in both good and bad ways. For example, if you take a run in your community every morning, a neighbor a few blocks down might recognize your habit of exercising and be encouraged to start exercising as well.

In the same way, if you lounge around in the lunchroom five minutes after your lunch break ends, you might notice a friend from work or your colleague doing the same.

Your habits can also change the lives of people you interact with on a regular basis, since they can adopt your behaviors without even knowing. So, habits build us as individuals, and as humans, we build each other.

Some good behaviors that friends, family and colleagues can adopt from you include

- being on time

- eating healthy

- being productive (people are less likely to procrastinate around someone who is being productive)

- having a healthy sleep routine

- being polite and helpful

- smiling and laughing more (smiles and laughs are contagious)

- being organized

- reading

- finishing a task before starting a new one

- exercising

- practicing meditation

- journaling

Conversely, habits can get personal. Your entire family may suffer as a result of your unhealthy habits. If you have kids, the effect is felt more greatly because they pick up the majority of their undesirable habits from their parents. You should make every effort to replace your poor habits with positive ones if you're a parent or model figure for kids, or a sibling, uncle or aunt—just about any model figure to someone else. Here are a few typical undesirable habits that others can adopt from you.

Poor Coping Techniques for Stressful Situations

By the time you reach adulthood, your response to stress in your life has likely become routine. Adults who were not taught healthy stress management techniques as children frequently use the negative coping skills they picked up from dependable adults. Ineffective coping mechanisms for stress include drinking, using drugs, smoking, or engaging in other forms of self-medication. Your children and others close to you may practice the same negative coping mechanisms.

Financial Irresponsibility

If you saw your parents spending money impulsively on things they didn't need while growing up, chances are good that you would do the same thing unless you become aware of it and stop it. Shopping impulsively or unnecessarily, overspending, and not having a solid handle on your finances may all have a bad influence on both you and your family. This also is why self-discipline is so important when establishing habits. They can also teach your kids risky practices.

Worry Compulsively

Kids will pick up on your persistent anxiety about things that you cannot control. They observe their parents, whom they have the utmost faith in to protect them, worrying about everything. Children who worry excessively also experience insecurity and may act out. If you wish to stop worrying, you might need to seek professional assistance, such as counseling—especially if anxiety runs in your family. Maintaining a daily self-care routine and engaging in meditation and exercise are other ways to quit worrying.

Having A Picky Diet

There are several causes of picky eating, such as physical and intellectual challenges, allergies, and sensory issues. Some individuals may also exhibit pickiness due to dietary constraints. However, some adults refuse to eat some foods simply because they are unpleasant. An excellent method to promote healthy eating habits over unhealthy ones that can make eating in social situations challenging in the future, is to encourage your kids to at least try new meals and provide these foods to them during mealtimes that are not stressful.

Not Expressing Yourself

Adults should never be hesitant to express themselves in mature ways, such as quietly discussing their feelings, addressing whichever topic they want, or expressing an opinion. Children, friends and family frequently learn to be nervous, dissatisfied, and frightened to be themselves—let alone fully express themselves—when adults are reluctant to express themselves. Children learn confidence and self-assurance via expression.

Having Problems Communicating

Lack of self-expression may be exacerbated by ineffective communication. Some people find it quite difficult to discuss their problems with others, even their relatives. Younger adults, kids or anyone you influence who don't observe adults interacting appropriately, will frequently mimic that behavior and become even more emotionally distant and withdrawn from their close relatives and friends. So, it is crucial that you practice being honest and upbeat with your family instead.

Having Trouble Maintaining Positive Relationships

It might be challenging to keep up positive ties with your family if you're unable to communicate, you worry excessively, or you always avoid conflict. You can build up solid relationship-building and maintenance skills by establishing healthy communication and listening skills, as well as positive interactions. When you demonstrate to your children or loved ones that you, for example, often go out to lunch with your best friend. They will learn that maintaining relationships with people outside of your immediate family is similarly essential for leading a good, balanced life.

Not Apologizing Enough

You may have heard jokes about people not being able to apologize, but this is not a nice attribute to have. If it describes you, start learning how to do it right away. It's simple. Just admit your error and follow it with a sincere apology. Being sincere in your apology is important, but your loved ones should be able to talk to you about what both you and they did and why it was wrong in a manner that stimulates their understanding.

Unhealthy Eating

Our connection with food is one of the most important habits we inherit from our parents. When you eat foods unique to one region or culture as a child, you often prepare those foods for your home and family. Parents who consume a lot of soda, junk food, and go out to dine regularly, send the message to their kids that eating poorly is normal and expected.

Without a doubt, the poor habits mentioned here have a detrimental effect on your family or those close to you. Even partners, coworkers or people in your community can pick up negative behaviors from one another, but recognizing your own poor habits is the first step to getting rid of them!

How An Accountability Partner Can Change Everything

Do you find it difficult to hold yourself accountable to your objectives and habit-forming goals? When you know no one is around to witness and you get distracted, do you ever find yourself compelled to watch Netflix or hesitant to finish your project for work?

If so, you're not alone. But there are a variety of strategies you can use to keep yourself on track and accomplish your objectives, while still striking a healthy work-life balance. One such strategy is having an accountability partner.

Having an accountability partner can be compared to a collaboration where both people commit to mentor and provide feedback on each other's performance over a predetermined period of time. Weekly or daily feedback exchanges are usually given, and this also helps you both stay on track with your habits and goals.

Why Is Having an Accountability Partner Important?

Of course, with self-discipline, your accountability partner can be yourself. This is internal accountability. However, we will focus on external accountability partners.

Working with an accountability partner can help with fostering new habits. It stands to reason that motivating people to work together toward a common objective is a necessary part of reaching any goal. When you're cut off from a group, achieving your goal could become difficult. But this isn't the only reason accountability partners are effective and beneficial to habit building.

You can get assistance from an accountability partner in creating new habits in the following areas:

- nutrition or dieting
- exercise training
- successful communication
- meditation and emotional development
- parenting

- relationships

- making a budget and saving

- organizing at home

- self-help

- learning and growth

- writing

The Advantages of an Accountability Partner

In addition to the good habits that accountability partners can help you establish, here are some more detailed advantages of having such a partner in your journey of habit building through self-discipline.

Keep You Inspired

People frequently lose motivation during any process of following a life goal. This is not something to be embarrassed about or afraid of because everyone experiences it, even the best of us. The entire process, though, might be derailed if you lose motivation at pivotal moments. In fact, a lot of people simply give up, which results in the failure of any goal they had in mind.

Accountability partners now join the conversation. They consistently inspire you by supporting you with their words and deeds. The impact that the correct words may have on your motivation is truly astounding. When you start to lose motivation, accountability partners don't give up on you; instead, they figure out ways to re-motivate you. That is wonderful.

Continuous Development

One of the very few aspects of life where there are no boundaries is improvement. Accountability partners are constantly looking for ways you can better yourself, so there is always room for progress, even after doing everything you aimed to do. Therefore, there is always room for improvement, even when what you've done is already amazing.

An accountability partner could accomplish this by providing an alternative view of what you accomplished. They might also merely examine the entire procedure carefully to find flaws and weak points in your work.

Helpful Support and Counsel

If you've ever completed a project from beginning to end, you'll appreciate the significance of help and counsel. There are often occasions when things start to get difficult and your judgment starts to blur. This is an extremely delicate situation, since, if not handled appropriately, it may mean the end of the project.

But that's what accountability partners are for. They simply never stop guiding and encouraging you during these difficult moments. You can succeed if you have the knowledge that someone is actively hoping for your success and demonstrating it through their actions.

Keep in mind that this help and guidance is not just for when you're feeling low. You need a person to celebrate with, even when you achieve significant victories and breakthroughs, such as if you quit smoking or exercise without putting too much energy into thinking about it.

Sincere Compliments

It might be challenging to receive honest criticism. When working on a project or program, people frequently surround themselves with their family and friends. The complete truth is sometimes withheld by your friends and family because they don't want to offend you or make you feel unhappy.

But you won't reach your potential or advance to the next level with your habit goals like that. If you allow them to "protect" you, they will maintain your mediocrity. On the other side, your accountability partners are interested in your real improvement. These collaborators will provide you with genuine critique on your progress, no matter how painful it may be. This straightforward criticism could mean the difference between success and failure.

Accountability Partner Qualities

Finding the right accountability partner is just as crucial as actually having one. It's important to remember that you don't want someone who will make you feel bad, because this will just make the situation worse.

Here are some qualities you should look for in an accountability partner if you're trying to locate the proper individual to keep you in check.

Disciplined

As we know from previous chapters, self-discipline is key. Everyone should be disciplined, and accountability partners aren't an exception. You must make sure that the partners you have are disciplined, since lack of discipline on their part may reflect poorly on you.

There are moments when we are down and require motivation. If your partner has the motivation to help you advance, they are the appropriate match for you, and your relationship will be successful. With a conversation and some encouragement, they can help relieve your stress and put you back on the correct track.

When it's time to put your goals into action, having an accountability partner who can inspire you will also help you avoid procrastination.

Challenging

Partners in accountability should not settle for mediocrity. They constantly want you to develop and get better. When you begin to let your guard down and fall behind, they push you to work more.

Always push yourself forward and be aware of your limitations. It will be quite advantageous for both of you if you and your accountability partner have the same mentality.

To avoid failure, it's essential to refrain from going overboard. The best course of action is to be aware of where you stand and use your accountability partnership as a foundation for progress.

Patience

Your accountability partner should be patient. They shouldn't make rash judgments, and shouldn't pressure you into making choices either. They are aware of the importance of exercising patience when making decisions, especially in urgent situations.

The willingness to engage in frequent and ongoing conversations is another critical quality in an accountability partner. Your partner should have the time and commitment to provide you with feedback on a daily or weekly basis. Additionally, it's critical to maintain continual accountability for all significant decisions you make.

Supportive

Supportive—naturally. An excellent accountability partner must constantly offer encouragement and words of support.

You should be on the lookout for this quality in your relationship since it's essential to have someone who genuinely cares about your well-being. They must have just your best interests in mind.

Your partnership will be detrimental and will just keep you farther away from your goal if the other party doesn't have the best intentions. This is much worse than being alone. Find someone who helps you become a more successful and better person.

Ability to Offer Criticism That Is Beneficial

Today, this quality is frequently overlooked. An accountability partner must be able to offer constructive criticism and honest feedback. Take note of the word "constructive" here. This implies that they should understand how to critique without demeaning the recipient.

An accountability partner with extensive experience might be a valuable asset. Experience allows them to predict whether a habit change will be successful or whether a new diet will be feasible.

Having someone like that on your side may be what makes you successful. You can use their experience to your advantage and further your goals.

Types of Accountability Partners

Now that we understand the fundamentals of who an accountability partner is, it's critical to be aware of the many partner categories you can pick from. This provides you the flexibility to choose someone who will suit your preferences or particular objectives.

Licensed Counselor

In any industry, consulting a specialist is always a fantastic approach to get advice. They have a great deal of experience, which you can use to reach your goals. They are skilled at assisting you in striking a balance between your desires and needs, as well as between your feelings and rationality.

Senior with a Comparable Journey

Having someone who has gone through similar things to what you are experiencing, might be helpful since they can offer you the right advice for success. It's possible that this individual is younger than you, but just has greater expertise in a particular field. They don't absolutely need to be older than you.

Colleague

Another excellent option for an accountability partner is a coworker who is on the same professional path as you and might share some of your interests. Having feedback from a third party who is impartial can help you better manage your career and thrive at work through better habits.

A Close Friend or Relative

Someone close to you is a terrific candidate for your accountability partner since they will constantly have your best interests at heart, and genuinely care about your achievement. Their suggestions and criticism are always for your benefit. Just make sure they are willing to be completely honest, even if it makes you feel uncomfortable for a moment.

How to Begin with a Partner Accountability

Finding someone who is equally passionate and committed to forming new habits is now your aim. Make a list of prospective people you can trust, and let them know what you intend to do. People you hold in high regard should be on the list.

As a word of advice, keep your close friends out of the relationship so that it doesn't devolve into idle conversation. Every action must be thought out and intentional. The key to a successful relationship is being open and honest with one another.

As a result, consider the following if you're prepared to engage with an accountability partner:

- Is the potential partner reliable? Can you count on the person to appreciate your advice and carry it out?

- Are they able to handle challenging conversations? Can you give honest critique without having to put up with frivolous justifications or defensiveness?

- Does this person have a more expansive vision for their life? Do they share your aspirations in some way?

- Is this person prepared to take action? Do they have a strong sense of dedication and are they willing to go above and beyond the norm?

Additionally, you might need to be honest with yourself and engage in self-reflection. Recognize your past shortcomings if you haven't always been dependable, honest, and dedicated.

You don't have to lie to yourself; strive to accept both your current situation and your aspirations for the future. You'll be able to concentrate on supporting your accountability partner's achievements as a result, because you can't give what you don't have.

Here are five steps to finding a partner for accountability:

Step 1: Locate the Proper Person

Who you meet depends on where you search. You can conduct a search offline or online. Attending local meetups, TEDx Sessions, or contacting serious friends who require an accountability partner, are some options.

You can also use the following platforms and tools

- blogs, websites, and forums that are related to the habits you wish to develop

- LinkedIn groups (type the habits to search for groups around them)

- applications for accountability like coach.me and MyFitnessPal

- Meetup groups and neighborhood events

- workshops and seminars

By committing to an accountability partner, you'll have an easier time working with generating prospects.

Step 2: Be Receptive to Potential Partners with Diverse Backgrounds

Work with a colleague who has comparable accomplishments but dynamic talents and flaws that are different from your own.

Physical development can be aided by doing things like eating healthily and getting regular exercise. If you've mastered the art of eating healthily but need motivation to start exercising regularly, find a workout partner who isn't as well-versed in healthy eating as you are. Together, you and your partner will produce fantastic results.

If you want to be challenged and held responsible in a way that is more productive than being coached, find someone who is more successful in the area where you need improvement. Each hour you spend together will help you grow closer and make it easier to form new habits.

Step 3: Meet Your Preferred Candidate

Once you've decided on one of the prospects from the list, ask the person if they are interested in forming an accountability partnership. Outline the fundamental principles, how it operates, and the advantages of the connection.

If either of you are unsure about having each other as an accountability partner, talk for a while and make your decision after getting to know one another.

Step 4: Determine the Date, Time, and Meeting Style

The meetup can be organized in a variety of ways. You can communicate updates over the phone, via Facetime, in person, via email, on social media sites, or via text message. It doesn't matter how you communicate as long as you provide mutual accountability.

You can agree on a time and date that works for both of you to ensure accountability. It's crucial to keep a regular routine as well. In order to attain consistency, both parties should evaluate their weekly routines and choose an appropriate time.

There's little doubt you might need to change the meeting time, but it's critical to set a regular time that fits into your calendar for the entire week. Every time you have a scheduled meeting, your mind can relay thoughts and problems that need fixing, so you can address them at the next meeting.

Step 5: Establish A Weekly Statement of Accountability

The next step is to draft what is referred to as "accountability state-ments." You both will carry out these concrete tasks before your next meeting. They resemble milestones; minor tasks that are a necessary component of a larger goal.

The letters PACT stand for:

- **P- Possible**: Are the goals outlined in the responsibility state-ment realistic and attainable? Even if it's a good idea to plan large, your objective needs to be reachable so that it may be carried out within the allotted time.

- **A- Action-based**: Can you carry out the objective? If you're able to perform this action, you're on the right track.

- **C- Clear**: Your accountability statement ought to make things clearer. It should not include any arguments against achieving the aim. It ought to be concise and straightforward.

- **T- Time-related**: You should include a precise due date for each commitment. The due date could be at the subsequent meeting. However, you might agree to interact online or agree to share results online if you both feel there will be a significant gap before the next meeting.

In Essence

The advantages of collaborating with an accountability partner when forming new habits cannot be overstated.

Simply ensure that you take the five steps mentioned above so you may both get the most out of your relationship.

Utilizing the PACT technique, concentrate on the issue that both of you are facing, give the other partner your honest opinion, and make an accountability statement.

If you can divide your main objective into smaller milestones, you'll develop new habits. Additionally, two smart heads are preferable to one. The most important goals can be accomplished more quickly through an accountability relationship than by going it alone.

Being Surrounded With the Right People

Everyone aspires to succeed in their career, finances, and interpersonal connections. Why then do so few individuals genuinely succeed in all of these areas?

The key is to get rid of those people that are negative and make you feel bad. Be with people who encourage you, share their wisdom with you, and help you learn from your failures. Raise the bar for those you surround yourself with.

This idea is also known as the law of attraction. The notion that you become the people you spend the most time with, has persisted for so long because it's accurate, and you can use it to realize both your professional and personal goals.

Why is it Important to Surround Yourself With The Right People?

Have you ever heard the phrase, "You are who your friends are?" If you're a parent, you probably worry about your children hanging out with the wrong crowd, just as your parents did for you. This is due to the fact that the people you interact the most with, have a significant impact on your moods, perspective of the world, and standards for yourself. Parents naturally understand this and want to use the power of closeness to positively influence their children. So why don't we, likewise, take advantage of it for ourselves?

Every area of your life, including your career and your relationships, can benefit from being surrounded by positive individuals. You're more likely to acquire empowering habits and believe that life is happening *for you* rather than *to you,* if you surround yourself with optimism. Similar to how being around joyful people makes you feel better, being around negative or closed-minded people in your professional or social circles makes you feel worse.

How To Surround Yourself with Good People

Power is in proximity: Always keep in mind that you become the person you spend the longest time with. You need to surround yourself with individuals who will challenge you while also inspiring you to succeed at new levels. Though it isn't always simple, it's worthwhile to attempt this.

Choose To Be Inspired by Greatness

Everybody has goals for their lives, but which ones are absolute necessities in your book? Your relationships and the activities you choose to spend time on are both reflections of your standards. Set higher goals for yourself, as this is the best way to start surrounding yourself with positivity.

It's possible that you've become accustomed to specific people's company or that you're anxious about moving on. Don't let fear dictate how you live. Once you realize that your objectives and desires are worthwhile, you'll be unstoppable.

Let Go of Negative Relationships

Yes, we've all heard this one before, I'm sure of it. Whether it was on TV, indirectly, from a family member or you read it somewhere, we've all heard of the danger of surrounding ourselves with negative people. Well, it's true.

Are those around you preventing you from achieving the next level of success? Making changes to your friendship group or colleagues starts with figuring out who in your life is causing you to feel negative.

Consider how you feel after being around these people, to get a better idea of who they are. Do you feel confident in yourself and up for a challenge? Or do you feel agitated, insecure in yourself, and emotionally uncontrollable? Our emotions are there to inform us; they're a gift that shows us what needs to change if we want to feel more content.

Moving on from failing relationships can sometimes be uncomfortable. You might have known a few of these friends or coworkers for a very long time, so you don't want to endanger such relationships. However, it's crucial to avoid feeling indebted, or as though you owe them anything, because they are "old friends." Find out why you choose to stay in these relationships so that you may alter your perspective and set yourself free. You'll be better equipped to concentrate on the things that are important to you.

Identify the Good People

You undoubtedly already have some positive relationships in your life, just as you probably have some unpleasant ones as well. They don't all need to be the same; in fact, having a variety of character traits within your group will be advantageous. When you want to associate yourself with positivity, it's a good idea to have these four kinds of individuals in your inner circle:

- **Smart individuals**. Being around brighter people will encourage you to continue learning and to be interested, two qualities that are crucial for anyone who wants to thrive in self-discipline.

- **Diligent workers**. Success is more than just being brilliant; in fact, there are many intelligent people who lack the motivation to succeed. Everyone around a hard worker is motivated to do more, be more, and accomplish more, and is inspired by their hunger.

- **Visionaries and dreamers**. Both doers and dreamers are essential to the world. The visionary in your group is the one who will consider your craziest suggestions and always inspire you to pursue your goals.

- **Believers in the good**. There are people who see challenges as opportunities and people who perceive them as insurmountable barriers, therefore no one is ever really satisfied. You want to surround yourself with the first type of person when times are bad.

Go Beyond Your Comfort Zone

Where your comfort zone ends, is where all growth begins. This is probably the very essence of habit-building. If you find like-minded people on the third floor of your business, but you're on the ninth floor, make the trip during lunch and breaks, to be with them. You must spend time where they are if you want to be surrounded by good people who will advance you.

Also, ambitious people go to seminars and workshops that challenge them intellectually and personally. They consistently step outside of their comfort zones and expose themselves to people with diverse viewpoints.

Role Models Like a Rock Star

Do you remember who your role model was when you were a kid? Did you have an 'idol' who you wanted to be like? Looking back now, would you still want to be like that person?

Your aspirations and objectives undoubtedly evolved a little bit as you grew older. Your closest relative, such as a parent, grandmother, sibling, or anyone else you found motivating, became your role model.

You probably have people in your adult life who you give credit to for helping you achieve the success you have. You would've struggled a lot more if they weren't there. Everyone receives some assistance along the way, but you have to work really hard for everything you currently have.

Everyone is entitled to a positive role model. Everybody needs assistance occasionally. People at any stage of life, in any field, can benefit from having someone to turn to. They support your growth and provide you with goals which to strive for.

Having a role model can be helpful no matter who you are or what you aim to do, even in habit breaking and building. For example, you may be struggling to break a habit of smoking, and you think it's impossible. But then you meet someone who did it, and they inspire you to try harder, seeing that it's indeed possible. This is the very essence of role models.

It can also assist you in serving as an example for the individuals in your life who you love and who you want to help improve their lives, when you, too, become a role model.

The following are some advantages of having a positive role model.

Role Models Instruct

Theoretically, a good role model is someone who excels in a field that you respect. You might wish to get better at fitness, business, your spirituality, or anything else.

An excellent role model can instruct you in many different ways. When you ask for assistance, they can provide it, and when you make mistakes or need guidance, they can provide helpful criticism.

They might not even be conscious of teaching. An effective role model leads by example. Simply put, they can demonstrate successful behavior and actions for you.

It's likely that you've heard the phrase "learn from your mistakes." That's true in certain instances, but you can also avoid the time and shame your role model experienced from following the wrong road by learning from their mistakes.

Role Models Inspire

Role models are crucial because they deliberately and unconsciously push you to rise to their level.

You're more likely to succeed if you're around successful individuals. It motivates you to work even when you don't want to, improve your health, and reach more objectives. It might even encourage a little bit of constructive competition.

People who are successful look to other successful individuals for inspiration. Everybody uses a distinct strategy to accomplish their objectives. It's tremendously informative to observe people you admire to learn how they achieve their goals.

Accountability is crucial at all times. An effective and long-lasting strategy to reinforce accountability is to have a role model you can look to for guidance and inspiration.

Pillar 5:

Process

It's funny how habits work. We use them blindly, putting our brains on automatic piloting and unconsciously settling into a comfortable pattern.

Once bad habits become ingrained in your brain, they are hard to get rid of, even with all the self-discipline in the world. Instead, replace bad habits with new ones, and make *those* stick. But how?

In this chapter, I discuss methods of creating routines and habits that stick.

Using Habit Reminders/Cues

Although the old adage that everything you do for 21 days will become a habit has largely been debunked, there is still some truth to it: anything you do for long enough will become an ingrained behavior. Some people develop habits more rapidly than others do, while others take longer to do so, but eventually the behaviors become second nature.

Therefore, creating effective habits requires repetition of a desirable behavior over an extended period of time until it becomes automatic.

But how can you keep that at the front of your mind?

Triggers Are Wonderful Because They Serve as Reminders

Anything you "place in your way" to remind you to perform a task is a trigger. The best triggers have some connection to the desired behavior.

For instance, you might put something in front of the door so that you have to pick it up before leaving your house, if you wish to remember to bring an item to work that you normally wouldn't.

However, a trigger can be anything that draws your attention and prompts you to take action. A good example is an alarm clock or timer.

Leave a trigger in your way to remind you to do whatever it's you're trying to turn into a habit, and leave it there until you notice you've already done it. This is the best way to establish a new habit. For instance, sticking a post-it note that reads "drink your green juice" on the refrigerator can help you remember that you should be reducing your intake of soda, until you finally discover that you're no longer in need of the reminder.

All of these triggers, however, need a lot of planning because you have to keep in mind why you need to recall something in the first place. The ideal reminder is often one that is fully automatic; you set it up, forget about it, and trust the trigger to activate when you need it.

Try these three easy types of reminders to help you start a new habit.

1. The Visible Prompt

Our physical surroundings are one of the unique things that can change how we act. According to the idea of behavior change, our environment can affect how we act and how we interact with each other without us noticing. Making something visually appealing to serve as a reminder to do a specific task, is a fairly easy way to keep yourself focused on your healthy habit or goal. This might resemble

- post-it notes on the mirror or refrigerator

- a written message for your workstation or desk

- a screensaver or wallpaper for a smartphone or PC

- setting out your workout attire the previous evening

- anything that will serve as a reminder for you to carry out the action throughout the day

2. The Technical Reminder

To keep yourself accountable for your new habit, set up a regular calendar or silent alarm. Consider adding a notification in the app on a smartwatch or portable device so it will buzz you into action!

Here is a list of habit apps to help:

- **Momentum Habit Tracker**: This app includes loads of helpful tools for monitoring habits and routines. Momentum Habit Tracker's import-to-Excel capability offers cross-platform viewing of your performance. Set weekly goals and take notes to simply manage your behaviors. The app is optimized only for Apple devices, hence it's not available on Android. However, your Momentum profile can be readily integrated on iCloud.

- **Habitica**: This app's approach to tracking positive habits is unique. Each activity you accomplish levels up your unique avatar, providing extra motivation. Its video-game-inspired design makes tracking habits and goals fun. You can join your friends and perform quests and missions with the app. Habitica may not appeal to non-gamers.

- **Productive Habit Tracker**: Do you want to track your habits? Then you should use this app. Productive Habit Tracker's simple, well-designed user interface simplifies habit tracking. This app's easy design lets you plan in seconds and the basic interface hides powerful features. This software tracks your achievements. So, you can track your development, and in turn, it motivates you.

- **StickK**: Yale behavioral economists created StickK. When you sign up, you make a commitment agreement between yourself and the app to attain your goals. Assign a friend or family member to examine your data for added motivation. The commitment contract notion could boost motivation. The app is built on Thaler's nudge theory, which is well-researched. The app's layout is also eye-catching.

- **Habitshare**: This app combines social networking and habit tracking. So you can form habits with friends. This makes it a top habit-tracking app. The platform's social features are rare, and unlike some others with social networking connections, this program provides messaging capabilities to converse with friends. You can motivate each other this way. Individual aspirations become meaningful teamwork. If users want more privacy, they can disable the app's social features. However, Habitshare lacks monthly task scheduling, which could be a deal-breaker for some.

- **Streaks**: This Apple innovation award winner helps you stay motivated by fostering a 12-day streak of positive habits. You can customize the user interface to your liking. It's also easy to combine with IOS's Health app. Together, you'll easily form healthy behaviors. The app will send a reminder if you fall behind.

- **Habit List**: This app is all about building good habits. This effective habit tracker helps you track your habits over time and understand your development. Establish a calendar of activities if you have a complex schedule or wish to complete specific tasks on specified days.

- **Balanced**: Encouraging healthy behaviors, Balanced helps you track your sleeping, exercise, and sitting time. Balanced is a healthy-habits-only app. It helps you focus on three things at once so you're not overwhelmed.

- **Simple Habit Tracker**: This app is among the best habit trackers and has many cool features. The app includes 200 pre-designed habits for inspiration. This app's attractive interface is a big motivator.

- **Habitbull**: This is one of the most feature-rich habit tracker apps, and its detailed tracking mechanism shows your progress. Habitbull can be used with Google Fit to improve fitness. Your data can be stored in the cloud, so you'll never lose it. This habit tracker may be too complicated for others.

- **Strides Habit Tracker**: A wonderful all-around habit tracker. The software is simple to use, so you can create good habits quickly. The program calculates if you'll finish a specified number of chores by a certain date, allowing you to customize your habits to your goals.

- **Coach.me**: A habit monitoring software that lets you hire a habit coach or a leadership trainer for extra fees. If you're able to afford it, hiring a coach could boost your objectives and productivity. You can acquire the skills you need through leadership and habit coaching.

- **42 Goals**: A basic app but with numerous features. It's optimized for web browsers, unlike similar programs. You can share your accomplishments with friends in the website's online community.

- **Habit - 21 day routine**: This app is based on the idea that it requires 21 days to create a new habit and pushes you to sustain one for 21 days. The app's layout is attractive. However, additional habits cost extra on the app.

- **Chains.cc**: Every time you adhere to your habit, your chain expands, assisting you in remaining motivated. The app is attractive and has a simple interface. It's available online and offline, so you can follow your habits anywhere. However it's not free, but affordable.

- **Done**: Done lets you monitor an activity numerous times a day and has other fantastic habit tracker features. With the app, you may track new and old habits. It's customizable, unlike many other programs. Premium (paid) version lets you export habit information as a CSV file or on Dropbox. The basic version only tracks 3 habits until you subscribe to premium.

- **Good Habits:** This app's intuitive design lets you track your habits' growth. The app shows your behaviors and chains. It's usable with Apple Watch and Today Widget. It's not really different from other apps, however. If you enjoy the design, you may have fun.

- **Habitify**: A stylish, easy to use, intricate and thorough app. Habitify helps busy people stay focused by highlighting the most important habits and tasks. Graphs and statistics indicate progress and habits. It also syncs across iOS devices. If you don't mind the few customizing choices, you'll adore it.

- **Sessions**: Sessions is a habit tracker for timing your daily activities. Its simple user interface is also attractive. You may organize your day and plan your routines by setting specified times for each task. Track your success as you create efficient habits and routines.

- **Morning Routine Habit Planner**: This app helps you focus on one habit at a time. Combining it with Siri enables hands-free operation, which is a unique feature. The app also contains motivational advice from successful people.

- **Persistence**: When it comes to motivation, this app wins. This software tracks your progress toward goals and shows if you're on track. This will help you determine when to push yourself and when to relax. This software offers many ways to track goals. You can also enter notes on your progress and habits.

- **Way of Life**: Billing itself as the "ultimate habit-building app", this habit tracker has several options for individuals who desire to control their routines. On first usage, customers are provided with an engaging tutorial to ensure they rapidly grasp and use all the major features, including the option to share progress on social media, export data as an Excel or CSV file, and archive fulfilled goals for a record of success. The tutorial helps with the layout's complexity.

3. The Social Reminder

When you have a friend to support you in making a healthy habit a reality, it's simpler to commit to it. If you tell a friend about your plans to develop a new, healthy habit, they could decide to join you! Consider scheduling a weekly lunch hour with a coworker, for instance, to ensure that you both get outside for a walk in the fresh air. At the absolute least, a friend will probably check in with you and inquire about your progress.

Habits all depend on our responses and reactions to the challenges we face in life. You'll be more driven to remain on track if you set up a few helpful reminders. But keep in mind that creating lasting habits requires more than just utilizing the top habit tracker or writing a list. To maximize the outcomes, the proper mindset and self-discipline must also be developed.

Defining The Routine

A habit is a regular, repeated action that you often perform unconsciously, like going to the gym every morning. While routines are deliberate ways of carrying out repeated actions in a predetermined order, such as making coffee, brushing teeth, dressing, and making the bed each morning. Routines frequently consist of numerous habits or steps taken in the direction of a specific objective. Routines and habits play a big role in our lives.

Even though we frequently confuse the terms "habit" and "routine," they actually refer to two different concepts. You may create effective routines and cultivate positive habits by understanding their meanings.

Various Consciousnesses

How conscious and purposeful you are determines how habits and routines differ from one another. A habit typically appears as an innate need to act, which is frequently sparked by a specific stimulus. The more deeply ingrained the habit, the greater the link between the trigger and the habit.

Routines, on the other hand, call for intentional practice. Making your bed every morning, hitting the gym, going on Sunday hikes, and meditating regularly are routines that should be continued consciously or else they eventually stop working.

Both routines and habits include repeating behaviors on a regular basis, but routines demand a higher level of intention and commitment than habits do. The foundation for forming positive habits and creating successful routines is self-control and self-discipline.

Routines can become habits with practice and the correct methods, but this process is neither automatic or unconscious. To make a routine become a habit, one must genuinely wish to do so.

The Importance of Routines

We know that habits are important, but do routines hold any significance? Why do we need them?

Routines Act as a Stabilizer

We can get anchored in daily life by routines. Comfort and stability are produced by eating breakfast at the exact time every morning and by eating dinner and going to sleep at around the same time every night. Life is easier to manage when we are on top of our routines. This feeling of control enables us to adapt to sudden changes.

Routines Provide a Map for Us

Routines also help to lower stress. Everyone has a "to do" list, or a list of things they want to get done in their daily or overall existence. Keeping this list bottled up in our heads can be exhausting. When our day is structured into a routine, we reduce the requirement for unnecessary mental effort since we are less likely to focus on each individual task that needs to be completed. By encouraging emotions of order and direction, it gives us a path to follow and reduces stress.

Routines Encourage Healthy Self-Care Behaviors

Routines assist us in developing healthy daily routines that encourage self-care. To sustain happiness and a sense of fulfillment, we can plan our time around the things we value most. We can make the time for activities that become a regular part of our routine, such as relaxing activities like yoga and meditation and getting to bed at a regular time to boost health.

Routines Foster Optimal Sleep Cycles

Just as crucial as establishing a morning routine, is having a good sleep regimen. Our mental, physical, and emotional health depend on getting enough sleep. Our bodies establish a sleep-wake cycle when we routinely go to bed and wake up at the same time. This cycle helps us fall asleep more easily, enhances the effectiveness of our sleep, and facilitates an easier awakening in the morning.

Routines Maintain Healthy Eating and Exercise Behavior

To maintain good emotional, mental, and physical wellbeing, we must adhere to appropriate eating habits and daily routines. Setting aside time each day to go grocery shopping, prepare meals, and cook is simple. Recipe research and culinary experimentation can even develop into an enjoyable hobby.

Due to varying interests, developing routines for fitness and physical exercise is a personal process. Some people enjoy participating in sports, while others enjoy doing yoga or working out in the gym. Individualized routines enable us to set priorities for the things that are significant to us and reserve time for them. As a result, we encourage our capacity to identify what drives us and engage in it often.

The Development of Ritual

We are able to cram all of our most crucial tasks into our days thanks to the consistency and individuality of our routines. This does not imply that we must follow a schedule when we start to feel trapped or bored, as doing so might be detrimental. A crucial component of development is learning to modify and improve upon our routines. We can enable our routines to change throughout time in reaction to change, which is a natural part of life.

When There Is No Routine

Routines provide structure and support emotional, mental, and physical well-being. Lack of routine frequently causes tension and feelings of not being in control. To deal with these emotions, many people turn to self-medication. Unfortunately, taking alcohol or narcotics to relieve daily stress can eventually result in addiction. Having a morning and nighttime routine can add structure to our erratic lives and shield us from negative stressors and impulses that might otherwise send us down harmful paths.

How To Make A Daily Routine In 6 Easy Steps

Whatever scheduling system you decide on, stick to these six steps to make a well-organized, lovely daily calendar.

1. Create A To-Do List

Make a list of everything you have to complete for the day before you organize your to-dos. You can either utilize a method like the Getting

Things Done (GTD) method to methodically record everything you need to do, or you can enter these items one at a time to your scheduling tool, so you know you've noted them.

Add recurring activities to your list, such as appointments, workouts, and meetings. Include sporadic responsibilities as well, such as phone calls or deadlines. You can choose how detailed to make your task list. To give structure to your day, for instance, feel free to make "go to lunch" a recurring task.

Tip: It's acceptable if you don't know all that needs to get done throughout the upcoming week. As new tasks come up, you may always add them to your list of things to accomplish.

2. Prioritize Your Work

If, after making your to-do list, you still feel overloaded, don't worry. Once you've prioritized, your checklist will feel more well-organized. You become more aware of what needs to be completed when you prioritize your tasks. In this manner, if it appears that you won't be able to complete all of your chores on a particular day, you can concentrate on the things that are most important, or those that are going to have the most impact.

Start by assigning each assignment a high, medium, or low importance to help you organize your work. When going through your chores, you can ask yourself a number of questions, such as

- Which projects have a strict deadline?

- Which duties must I finish on particular days?

- Which tasks, if not finished immediately, will cause me stress?

- What assignments do I want to finish first?

- What activities can wait?

Consider which task is more urgent if you have activities that conflict with one another.

3. List Due Dates

If you haven't already, check each item on your to-do list to see if it has a due date. Choose a deadline that sounds plausible for now if you're unsure about what the deadline ought to be; you can always adjust it later.

Similar to priorities, deadlines outline which tasks are most crucial and the due dates for completion. And although you might have ample time to complete a task, you risk forgetting it if there are no clear deadlines. In actuality, imprecise procedures are the second biggest cause of missed deadlines.

Reminder: Projects at work are not the only ones with deadlines. To hold yourself accountable, you might set your own deadlines for individual chores.

4. Recognize Recurrent Occurrences

Once you've highlighted the due dates on your to-do list, be sure to draw attention to any recurring occurrences. Weekly staff meetings, a monthly book club, or client phone calls are a few examples of these occasions.

Then, incorporate recurring events into your daily schedule. You won't have to remember to reschedule things every week or month if you do it this way.

Tip: Conducting a brief assessment of your regular events is also a smart idea right now. Are there any regular tasks you perform that you should stop or assign to someone else?

5. Sort Items by Deadline, Priority, or Time.

It's time to organize your to-do list by day and time now that the big moment has arrived. You can also arrange your things according to other criteria, such as priority or deadline.

Consider the actions you took above as you place the order for the things you desire. Your top priorities should be handled first, and your lower priorities can wait until later during the day or week. Distribute your recurring events appropriately throughout your calendar template. Your daily schedule will expand as your to-do list gets smaller.

To check how filled your calendar is, switch your to-do list to month view. You can add another step to the scheduling procedure if it appears that your schedule is already too packed. Remove any tasks you don't feel are essential so you have time to recuperate or make adjustments.

6. Remain Adaptable

You may start working on your daily routine now that you have a clear picture of it. It's crucial to maintain flexibility during the day and week since the items on your first itinerary are probably not what actually transpire.

Life is erratic and difficult to manage. Deadlines will change, and your regular Monday meetings might move to Wednesdays. When you have the ability to easily update your daily calendar, these adjustments will be less stressful.

Consider using a project management program as a standalone tool for scheduling. Organization, personalization, and visualization are the main focus areas of most forms of project management software. You can create a practical and adaptable daily routine if you make use of these elements.

Three Methods to Set Up Your Daily Agenda

Your daily schedule can be organized in a variety of ways. When working, you could choose to concentrate on a timetable or be more task-oriented.

Hourly

A daily schedule is typically set out using an hourly planner. Use the methods above to set times for your critical chores to create an hourly schedule. Each aspect of your day will have a clear framework thanks to this timetable. Additionally, you can plan for responsibilities away from work, such as a personal doctor's visit after work.

By Importance

You can prioritize your responsibilities in a list and work your way through the day from this list if you want an untimed daily routine. Even though this to-do list appears to be straightforward, you'll still need to tweak it to reflect your priorities for the day ahead. For instance, depending on the meetings, errands, activities, and appointments scheduled for that day, your priorities may alter.

By Deadline

Organizing your agenda according to due dates might give your day a sense of urgency. You can decide what should be placed first in your personalized planner by looking at the projects that are due. Your deadlines list will change every day, just like your list of priorities. You must review your list every morning and add any recurrent or irregular commitments.

Creating Your Reward Plan

What would it feel like if you begin a new habit, only to give it up in frustration after a short while?

Unfortunately, many people who desire to get more done, be more productive, or continue with an exercise program frequently have this problem.

What causes this to occur? People find it difficult to maintain consistency when they don't notice quick outcomes from their behavior modification, which is one reason why they struggle.

Fortunately, there is an easy method for maintaining your routines, objectives, and tasks. When you hit a significant milestone or complete a particular task, treat yourself. When you feel unmotivated—or are simply too exhausted to get started—it's simpler to maintain a habit if you have something to look forward to.

The Significance of a Reward System

Some might think that having a reward system for habit building is insignificant and might even be tempting if your reward is something unhealthy like a chocolate bar or tub of ice cream. But think about everyday life. Most things we do have a reward system that motivates us to do it. Even if we have a job that we looked forward to in the very first week, after a while, that excitement diminishes, and we need something else to drive us forward.

Habits are just the same.

Our initial drive to build new habits will diminish after a while, and it's going to be difficult to continue our mission with having nothing to look forward to. In fact, a 2018 study found that rewards were more effective than intrinsic motivation and the repetition of an action (Judah et al., 2018). Having a reward system contributes significantly to habit formation.

Here are some pointers for developing your own reward scheme:

- Find a balance that will enable you to improve as a person. While rewarding yourself is good, a system that is excessively generous won't work to help you achieve long-term changes. While creating your rewards system should be enjoyable, it's important to regularly assess if it will ultimately be beneficial.

- Examine your vices to find prizes that could be earned: What vices do you most frequently participate in, feel most tempted to do, or feel guilty about doing? These tasks might serve as the highest incentives. Additionally, guilt is an unpleasant emotion that you should deal with because it may indicate that a vice isn't worth your time and effort.

- Reward yourself for avoiding unhealthy behaviors. You might wish to stop engaging in some behaviors that you don't want to use as incentives. For each day that you don't overeat, for instance, you may give yourself two points.

- Pay attention to the behaviors that need to become automatic. It would be meaningless to treat yourself because you've made it a habit to read for a few hours each day. Points should take work to earn.

- Reward yourself based on the amount of work needed. For the amount of work you put into the system as a whole, you ought to treat yourself. Change your list or give yourself less habit points as your habits take hold—which will happen quite quickly—to keep the effort you invest in the system consistent.

- Concentrate on your best practices. The habits that have the greatest positive impact on other areas of your life are the most beneficial. Make these habits the focal topic of your scoring system.

Different Rewards

Depending on who you are and the types of habits you want to break or gain, there are different types of rewards that you may permit yourself. For example, if you're trying to quit drinking, perhaps the smoothie reward would be better than having a night out with your friends at the bar. Below is a list of types of rewards with examples.

Entertainment rewards:

- Visit a nearby comedy club to have fun. (Watching successful comics, in fact, is a terrific way to hone your sense of comedy.)

- Visit a festival, carnival, or arts and crafts exhibition.

- Attend a concert.

- Visit a gallery of art.

- Get a season pass to the opera or the theater.

Food rewards:

- Have a delicious smoothie.

- Purchase your favorite cake or pastry.

- Make your favorite meal. Use all those pricey components.

- For a few weeks, treat yourself to a meal delivery service instead of cooking.

- Take a sip of wine, or two!

- Dine at a restaurant you've always loved.

Free rewards:

- Make a call to, or spend the day with, a friend or relative who makes you happy.

- Color. Check out some enjoyable selections for adult coloring books.

- Create a private haven. Make a retreat at home where you can unwind.

- Sing and dance.

- Set aside a day to be lazy and accomplish nothing.

- Play a word search or crossword puzzle.

Self-Care rewards:

- Schedule a personal training session.

- Get your nails or feet done (or both).

- Get a new haircut or experiment with a different hair color.

- Get a new piercing or tattoo.

- Have a spa day.

- Practice some DIY self-care routines from home.

- Visit a running store to get fitted for exercise footwear.

Shopping rewards:

- Start a "rewards savings" account. Give yourself a financial reward. Add $5, $10, or $20 to your "rewards savings" account each time you accomplish a goal.

- Start collecting something, whether it be sports memorabilia, action figures, or stamps. Enjoy the excitement of collecting things and adding to your collection.

- Stickers will make your goal calendar more colorful. Stickers can be used to emphasize deadlines and celebrate accomplishments.

- Visit a thrift store, flea market, or antique store. You might eventually locate the very piece of furniture you've been hunting for.

- Purchase a big-screen TV, a car or home stereo, or both. Save this reward only for when you accomplish important objectives.

Outdoors and travel rewards:

- Get a dog as a pet and a strolling companion.

- Build a fire and take pleasure in its cozy warmth.

- Find a popular tourist destination or local hangout that you haven't had the chance to visit.

- Take a leisurely stroll in the park in the morning.

- Go on a pleasant hike by yourself, or with some friends.

- Visit a botanical garden and take in the flowers.

By rewarding yourself, you feel inspired to continue the habit training, so you can continue to grow and receive the ultimate reward of replacing bad habits with new ones.

The Value of Commitment Devices

Commitment devices are a voluntary decision you make now that will influence future decisions; you strive to limit future decisions to only those that represent your long-term goals. You must therefore be conscious of the times and places where your intentions and deeds diverge. So, commitment devices can also provide a penalty for deviating from your declared goals and objectives.

Commitment devices are choices you make today, when you have a "cool head," to bind yourself and prevent you from doing something bad later, when you have a "hot head."

Speaking of binding oneself, here is a quick fun story.

Greek mythology has one of the earliest and most well-known examples of commitment devices. Greeks were aware that the sirens' music would tempt sailors to perish. However, with his ship's mast chained to him and his crew's ears plugged with wax, Ulysses was the first person to hear the Sirens' singing without dying.

Commitment devices have been shown to increase gym attendance, help smokers stop by 40%, and improve medical adherence rates, among other positive outcomes (Salzer, 2022).

Commitment Devices Examples

We frequently overlook how small changes in our decisions today can help us commit our future selves to desired goals. Potential commitment devices are all around us. For instance, we can

- plan workouts with a companion (if you wish to work out more)

- invest on smaller lunchboxes (if you wish to eat less)

- subscribe to a fruit and vegetable delivery service (if you wish to eat and snack healthier)

Commitment Device Types

The types of commitment devices help to determine which commitment devices are more beneficial for a certain individual or circumstance.

Social

A commitment tool that increases the social cost of acting inconsistently with the long-term objective. Excellent for a person who values social responsibility.

Friction

A commitment tool that raises the trouble cost of acting inconsistently with the long-term objective. Excellent technique to alter the interior design of your home or place of business.

Financial

A commitment tool that increases the financial cost of acting inconsistently with the long-term objective. Money losses are never enjoyable. Not the right kind of commitment tool for anyone with a gambling addiction.

What Does a Commitment Device NOT Do?

Some behavior change techniques that are related to one another are sometimes mistaken for commitment devices. While they all entail voluntary commitments, they do not always entail the addition of restrictions, or higher costs for failing to act in accordance with long-term objectives.

- Pre-commitments: I promise to act in X way.

- Temptation bundling: I promise to perform X only when doing Y.

- Implementation goals (If/Then Plan): If event Y happens, then I'll take action on plan X.

While not Commitment Devices, they can all be effective behavior modification strategies, such as scheduling time blocks in your calendar (pre-commitment), restricting your favorite podcast to the gym (temptation bundling), or having a backup jogging schedule in case of bad weather (implementation intention).

Pillar 6:

Methods

Behind every behavior assessment, there are theories and principles to get you on the right track. Habits and self-discipline are no different.

In this chapter, we will discuss some of the various theories and principles that you can utilize to get you on the right track with your habits.

Pareto Principle

What do you do first when you enter the office in the morning? Most people grab their preferred coffee, check their email, and list their daily priorities. What methods do you employ, though, to prioritize your tasks?

The Pareto principle, sometimes known as the 80/20 rule, is one popular strategy. You may increase your productivity during the day by using this strategy to identify and prioritize your tasks with the greatest potential for impact. This can indirectly be a wonderful way to build routines and habits.

In other words, only a small proportion of causes result in disproportionate effects. Understanding this idea is crucial because it will enable you to decide which projects to prioritize in order to have the biggest impact.

What is the Origin of the Pareto Principle?

Vilfredo Pareto, an economist from Italy, created the Pareto principle in 1896. Pareto noted that only 20% of the population in Italy held 80% of the land. He also saw this to be the case with the plants in his garden, where 20% of the plants produced 80% of the fruit. The easiest way to quantitatively represent this relationship is as a power law distribution across two quantities, where a change in one number causes a meaningful change in the other.

Additionally, this theory has a few other names:

- Pareto principle

- The 80/20 rule (most common)

- Law of the vital few

- Principle of factor sparsity

The 80/20 rule is more of a general theory that may be seen in business, time management, economics, and even sports, than a rigorous mathematical equation.

Examples of the Pareto Principle in General

Though not necessarily related to habits, here are a few examples of the 80/20 rule to better explain it:

- 80% of a plant's fruit is found in 20% of the plant.

- 20% of a company's consumers account for 80% of its profits.

- 80% of the points are scored by 20% of the players.

In essence, this principle is saying that only 20% or *input* yields 80% of *output*. How can we relate this to habits and self-discipline? Well, say for example, you invest a small amount of your time every day to exercising. In 5-6 months, the improvements and changes you'll notice will be greatly impacted by that small, committed input in daily exercise. Even if you sit in an office for the majority of the day, your result will still be significant due to the 20% of effort that you invested in day-to-day exercising.

Application of the 80/20 Rule

While the Pareto principle is frequently employed in business and economics, the 80/20 rule is practically universally applicable. This is due to the fact that the 80/20 rule can assist you in deciding where to concentrate your efforts in order to maximize your productivity.

The Pareto principle can assist you in determining which section of any piece of work is the most influential if it can be divided into smaller portions.

Here are a few illustrations of actual uses for the tool.

Productivity

The 80/20 rule might help you prioritize the things you need to perform during the day.

20% of your total job list should be completed, according to the theory, in order to make 80% of the effect you can that day. Decide which duties will have the biggest impact on your team and concentrate on these for the day, in order to have the biggest impact.

Make a list of everything you need to complete in the day to accomplish this. The most impactful of those tasks should then be determined. Do any of your tasks need teamwork with other members? Do you currently have any responsibilities that are preventing projects from moving forward? These jobs might seem straightforward, but they have a big impact on the rest of the team, since they keep the process moving.

Making Choices

When solving problems, the Pareto principle can assist you in coming to the most optimal conclusions. The Pareto principle might assist you in setting priorities for change strategies when there are numerous reasons for a single issue. The process for doing this is as follows:

- Determine the issues that you're facing. These are the matters you're attempting to resolve through this decision-making process.

- Determine the root causes of these issues. Find every factor behind the hurdles you're attempting to fix, using a method like the 5 Whys process.

- Sort your issues into groups based on similarity. If some of these problems can be divided into similar groups, use this as a chance to put together a list of their causes. This might assist you in determining whether one solution can address several problems.

- Based on the effect on your habit process, give each of these issues a value. The value might simply be a number between 1 and 10, or it can be a monetary amount to denote the significance.

- Make a plan to focus on the top 20% of issues that have the most impact on the habit process. One solution is meant to tackle a number of difficulties at once, so then figure out which ones are in the top 20%. Once you know what the main problem is, you can make a plan to use problem-solving skills and come up with a solution that will get you 80% of your desired outcome.

Quality Assurance

Imagine you're investing your time and energy into something, but the negative impact outweighs the positive ones. With the 80/20 rule, your benefits should have the most weight, from the "20%" of effort you put in. So, if the quality of your habit process is not up to standard, you know there is something to be changed.

Benefits of Implementing the Pareto Principle

The primary benefit of applying the Pareto principle is that it allows you to accomplish more with less effort. You may be able to operate more productively and maintain focus on particular habits as a result.

By prioritizing activities correctly, you may use the 80/20 rule to increase your rewards more quickly.

The Pareto principle also has the following advantages:

- It clearly defined objectives.

- It results in a productivity increase every day, or most days.

- It gives you the capacity to divide your goal into doable chunks.

- It provides you with a more targeted approach.

Disadvantages of Applying the 80/20 Rule

The Pareto principle, which states that 80% of results may be attained with 20% of the labor, is frequently misunderstood. The 20% and 80% numbers refer to the causes and effects you're working on, not the amount of effort you're putting in. The objective is to concentrate your effort on a certain area of work to have a greater impact, rather than to minimize the amount of effort. To get 80% of the benefits, you must still invest 100% of your work into that 20% of focus.

The 80/20 rule has another drawback in that you can become overly focused and lose sight of other duties. Things can get lost if you just concentrate on the crucial activities and ignore the less crucial ones. The trick is striking the correct balance between following the 80/20 rule, and finishing the remaining tasks, even if they don't produce 80% of the results.

Morita Therapy

A practical and profoundly spiritual method to promote human well-being is Morita Therapy. It incorporates a number of concepts from Eastern philosophy and Japanese psychology, offering those in the West a fresh and potentially helpful perspective on issues such as existential dread, anxiety, and depression (Eggshell Therapy and Coaching, n.d). The foundation of Morita treatment is the acceptance of our true selves. The majority of Eastern ideologies, like Morita Therapy, support communal principles over individualistic ones.

Morita Therapy: What Is It?

Shoma Morita, a Japanese psychiatrist, created the Morita therapy to treat a wide range of anxiety-related issues, including depression, panic attacks, OCD, and generalized anxiety disorder (Kitanishi & Moric, 1995). The founder of Morita Therapy claims that this method of self-development works best for those who possess traits that cause them to be:

- anxiety-prone

- introverted and introspective

- detail-oriented

- hypersensitive to pain

- perfectionistic

- self-critical

- of a high-achieving mindset

- in search of achievement and acceptance from others

- aiming to prevent embarrassment and rejection

Personal development, such as building good habits, requires being conscious of one's thoughts and actions. The characteristics listed, however, can cause people to become so consumed with self-examination that it becomes crippling. When under stress, highly sensitive individuals may feel as though everyone is looking at them or criticizing them. They also have a tendency to be too critical of themselves. Due to their paranoia, they avoid social situations and use maladaptive coping mechanisms in an effort to manage their anxiety.

The natural tendency of our untrained mind is to push away emotions like fear, sadness, and worry through denial, avoidance, and suppression. Therapies that promote labeling particular feelings as "bad" only serve to strengthen this propensity. In the process of habit building and breaking, we sometimes grow stressed or frustrated when we fall back into an undesirable habit. Morita therapy, on the other hand, asserts that every emotion has a purpose. It's advised that we accept anxiety as a normal state of being and not put too much effort into consciously trying to regulate it.

Is Morita Therapy Successful?

Numerous conditions have been successfully treated with Morita Therapy. However, establishing it as one of the evidence-based psychotherapies would require many more clinical trials.

Despite the fact that Morita Therapy was primarily used to treat anxiety and obsessive-compulsive disorder, it's now used to treat a wide range of psychological conditions, including the following:

- Ongoing Depression

- Borderline Personality Disorder

- Bulimia

- Chronic Pain

- PTSD

- Addictions to drugs and alcohol

- A low sense of self

- Parenting and family issues

- Fear and nervousness over a better life

Morita therapy advises us to embrace anxiety as a normal state of being and to refrain from exerting undue effort in trying to regulate it. Our desire to live meaningful lives is reflected in our stress levels.

Keep Your Natural Emotions Uncontrolled

Experiential avoidance is seen in Morita treatment as the root of anxiety. The attempt to control or overcome fear turns into a problem, but acceptance—not complacency—is the answer. There are no right or wrong emotions in Morita Therapy. Any attempt to repress, ignore, or stigmatize emotions will keep us caught in a cycle. The purpose of this therapy is to teach us how to experience feelings rather than try to fight them. We can better prepare ourselves to deal with the problems of life by learning to recognize and live with our natural inner states.

Regardless of How You Feel, Take Constructive Action

We don't have to "embrace" our emotions in order to go on with our lives when using Morita Therapy. The easiest strategy to deal with anxiety is to get involved in enjoyable activities or put your full attention into getting the job done. Our thoughts will change from self-preoccupation to meaning-making when we accomplish this, which is important for habits. We start to understand that fear may coexist with action when we have an integrated experience of being productive day after day, task after task, despite the dread. This frees us from the cycle of helplessness and frustration. This idea shares many similarities with Acceptance and Commitment Therapy.

Traditional vs Modern Uses of Morita Therapy

Even though Morita Therapy has changed over the years and the original version is no longer frequently used, you might be interested in learning more about its history. Morita Therapy is typically exclusively used in a hospital setting. The four steps of the treatment, which could last a few weeks to many months, are as follows:

Step 1: Rest, Low Verbal Interaction, and Isolation

During the first stage, the client refrains from engaging in any physical activities other than going to the toilet and taking a bath. They have to be aware of their deepest sensations and thoughts. The client is experiencing the whole gamut of emotions at this point, and the therapist is not actively conversing with them. The major objective of the therapist is to watch while the client processes emotions free of extraneous distractions.

Step 2: Minimal Repetitive Work

Morita was alarmed by the frequent confinement of those suffering from anxiety and other mental illnesses. He understood the value of spending time in a natural setting to sharpen one's mind. Because of this, he suggested that in the second stage, clients be required to perform simple, repetitive tasks in nature that they find interesting, such as gardening (planting, weeding, and raking), bird watching, and woodcarving. Keeping clients engaged in simple chores encourages productivity and has a calming impact.

Step 3: Community Involvement and Work

Morita had the opinion that emotional depression and repetitive, tough work are incompatible. The client is now encouraged to engage in conversation with others, but only regarding the current task. In addition, the client is urged to keep a journal, which the therapist reads through.

Step 4: Exchanges With the Outer World

The client is more capable of coping with the outside world at this point and has a new viewpoint on how to do so. Negative emotions gradually become less frequent as the client keeps their attention on productive behavior.

When traditional Morita Therapy is not an option, outpatient therapy can nevertheless achieve experiential learning through role-playing, in-depth introspection, and guided experiential exercises like visualizations and meditation.

Although the "classic" Morita Therapy, which required a residential intensive, is no longer used, the guiding principles of the therapy are more important than ever. Morita therapy was created at the beginning of the 20th century. In Japan, a lot of people use Morita Therapy to alleviate their anxiety and sadness, and so can we.

If-Then Plans/Framework

If-Then planning is an amazingly simple method that you can start incorporating into your life right away. If-Then planning is a type of conditional planning that helps reduce the number of decisions that need to be made and assists you in overcoming any roadblocks that stand in the way of achieving your goals.

The formula for if-then planning looks like this: if event X takes place, then I will carry out activity Y.

We can examine the example of the fitness center to illustrate how it all works. The goal is to work out on a more regular basis.

- Detailed Objective: Attend the gym at least three times every week..

- Using the If-Then method: IF today is Tuesday, Thursday, or Saturday, THEN I'm going to go to the morning gym class.

- Alternate strategy number one: If I'm feeling really fatigued, I'll put on my workout gear and try to take it easy during class.

- Alternative strategy number two: IF I have a meeting on Tuesday morning and am unable to go to the gym, THEN I will attend the 5:30 session after work.

By putting together a backup strategy, you may avoid making decisions that aren't essential, which will make it much simpler for you to overcome the typical challenges you face.

In a nutshell, you stick to your positive routines and keep working at achieving your objectives.

A Guide to the Formulation of Your If-Then Plans

How exactly does one go about formulating an If-Then plan?

The following are the nine steps involved in putting this plan into action:

1. One Pattern of Behavior at a Time

In spite of everything, you should never try to change more than one habit at a time, especially if the habits are completely unrelated to one another.

2. Set a Target Goal

A goal ought to be a high-level concept of what it is that you want. It should be as specific as is humanly possible. It's not a smart objective to say "I want more sleep," but "I want to go to bed at 9 p.m. each night, in order to get eight hours of sleep " is exactly what you should aim for.

3. Create Mini-Goals

Every significant objective should be broken down into a number of more manageable milestones. These will keep you motivated, while also keeping your attention on the tasks that need to be completed. These are not only necessary for your overall success, but they will also help you cope with the specific triggers that often come up when you work towards a large goal. This is why they are so vital.

4. Set a Baseline

Without a solid foundation, it will be difficult to accomplish what you set out to do. If you find that you're spending an excessive amount of money, for instance, you should begin by keeping a record of your day-to-day expenditures. Examine where the money is going and what it is that you're normally purchasing to get a better idea of where it's going.

5. Identify Where Your Thoughts Come From

Take some time to reflect and evaluate the habit you're trying to break. When do you do it? What causes you to feel the need to do it? Are there some people in your life who influence you to engage in undesirable behavior? It will be easier for you to write effective if-then statements if you collect the maximum amount of data possible.

6. Keep a Record of Your Undesirable Habit

Bring a notebook with you everywhere you go for the next few weeks. Write down the stimuli that are around you whenever you have the thought of engaging in a negative habit. There are a variety of stimuli, including sights, sounds, smells, and even other individuals, that might operate as triggers. You'll eventually be able to formulate if-then sentences such as the following: "If I am at the diner, then I will only carry $40 in cash and nothing else."

7. Develop a Replacement Habit

The natural world despises empty spaces. If you're working toward breaking a negative pattern of behavior, you'll need to find a replacement for that behavior. It's much simpler to find a positive habit to replace an undesirable habit, rather than attempting to get rid of the habit completely.

As an illustration, let's imagine that you come to the conclusion that your habit of spending money is the way that you relax and relieve stress. You may replace it with a habit that involves physical activity. Consequently, you would formulate a statement of the kind "If I feel like purchasing something from eBay, I will go for a thirty-minute walk instead."

8. Set a Firm Commencement Date

If you put things off indefinitely, they will never get done. Don't do that. Determine when you'll begin your new habit. You're free to continue making improvements to both your approach and your assertions as you move forward.

9. Make Use of Past Mistakes to Improve the If-Then Plan

Failure happens. Don't let it get you down. If you're unsuccessful, simply add more suggestions to the list of ideas for your claims. What was the reason for the failure? Was there a particular cue or trigger for the habit that you failed to notice at first? What are some options for the next time?

It's likely that on your first try to break a habit, you won't be successful 100% of the time. In point of fact, it's in your best interest to anticipate failing at some point along the way. People who are successful over the long term are those who understand that making a single error does not spell the end of their fortunes. They make an effort to lessen the harm, combat the "what the hell" effect, and get back on the horse as quickly as possible.

Conclusions Regarding the Use of If-Then Plans

Developing a set of If-Then statements pertaining to your habits, is an effective strategy for creating changes that are long-lasting.

Make a plan for how you'll react in a variety of situations, and refer to this plan whenever you're confronted with the want to give in to a negative desire. When you have a detailed set of instructions for each and every circumstance, you'll discover that it's much simpler to keep the promises you've made to others.

The Hawthorne Effects

The phrase "Hawthorne effect" describes the tendency of some people to work more and perform much better when they're participants in an experiment. This tendency was first observed by Charles Hawthorne (Cherry, 2020). The term is frequently used to imply that individuals' behaviors may change, not as a result of any alteration of independent variables, but rather as a result of the attention they are receiving from researchers. This is a common usage of the term.

In psychology textbooks, particularly those related to industrial and organizational psychology, the Hawthorne effect has received a significant amount of coverage and discussion. But new research suggests that some of the early claims regarding the impact may have been exaggerated (Cherry, 2020).

Subsequent Research

Research conducted much later on the Hawthorne effect revealed that the initial findings may have been exaggerated in their significance. In 2009, researchers from the University of Chicago reanalyzed the original data and discovered that other variables also played a role in efficiency and that the effect that was originally described was, at best, weak. They also found that the relationship between productivity and the original factor was weak.

In addition, researchers discovered the original data from the Hawthorne trials and discovered that many of the later published claims about the outcomes are simply not supported by the data (Holden, 2008). This is a significant finding since it suggests that the claims may have been exaggerated. They did, however, identify examples of a probable Hawthorne effect that were of a milder nature.

A systematic review that was conducted in 2014 and published in the Journal of Clinical Epidemiology, discovered that research involvement effects are real, despite the findings of some more studies that were unable to establish strong evidence of the Hawthorne effect. After reviewing the findings of 19 separate investigations, the researchers came to the conclusion that these effects unquestionably take place. Despite this, the researchers believe further study is needed to understand the mechanisms, consequences, and causes of these impacts (Cherry, 2020).

Alternate Interpretations

It's possible that the Hawthorne effect has some bearing on how participants behave in trials; however, it's also possible that there are other factors that contribute to similar shifts in behavior. The following are some of the potential elements that could affect advances in productivity:

- **Demand characteristics**: When conducting studies, researchers will occasionally provide participants with oblique hints that help them know what the researchers are looking for. As a consequence of this, individuals will adjust their conduct in order to assist the experimenter in validating their hypothesis.

- **Effects of novelty**: It's possible that the fact that researchers were watching people's behaviors also played a part. This may result in an immediate boost in performance and productivity, but over the course of the experiment, those improvements may eventually level off.

- **Performance feedback**: In circumstances concerning the productivity of workers, higher attention from the researchers also led to an increase in the amount of performance feedback received. It's possible that the greater feedback will actually lead to a rise in overall productivity.

Although the Hawthorne effect has frequently been exaggerated, it's still a helpful concept to have because it provides a basic explanation for the psychological aspects that can influence how people behave in an experiment.

Methods to Lessen the Impact of the Hawthorne Effect

It's vital to eliminate potential difficulties and sources of bias like the Hawthorne effect in order for researchers to have faith in the outcomes of tests. This effect refers to the phenomenon in which one variable is measured more frequently than another. Therefore, what can researchers do to reduce the impact of these effects in the experiments that they conduct?

- An experiment in natural settings and the use of naturalistic observation techniques can help get rid of or reduce certain sets of data and other possible sources of experimental bias. However, unfortunately, this is not something that can be guaranteed.

- Making the respondents' answers in an experiment fully anonymous is another strategy for overcoming this type of prejudice. It's possible that the participants' behavior won't change as a direct result of participating in a study if it's conducted in this manner.

Despite the fact that many of the initial conclusions of the Hawthorne experiments have since been proved to be either exaggerated or incorrect, the phrase has still become commonly used in psychology, economics, business, and a variety of other fields. More recent research lends credence to the notion that these effects do in fact take place; however, it's unclear how much of an influence they truly have on the results. Even in modern times, people frequently use this term to refer to changes in behavior (such as habits) that can occur as a direct result of participating in an experiment.

Pillar 7:

Measure

In the end, all this would be pointless if you're all over the place with your progress. In particular, if the goal is significant to you, setting both personal and professional goals can boost productivity and give you a sense of accomplishment. Setting good goals requires measuring your progress, because it may be used to prioritize tasks and determine how long they might take to achieve. Monitoring your development can also assist you in figuring out how to modify your plan of action, which might hasten your advancement.

In this final chapter, we discuss the significance of progress assessment, describe how to assess your own progress, and offer concrete examples of its application.

Measure Your Progress

Measuring your progress can help you get closer to your goal after you've set one. It can aid in your understanding of the ways that work best and the kinds of actions that advance you. You can then include these techniques into your overall approach for achieving your good habits and self-discipline. How far you have to go to reach a goal can be determined by tracking your progress. This could serve as a motivational reminder of what you're attempting to accomplish.

How to Evaluate Your Success

Consider taking the following actions to accurately measure your progress:

Determine Your Goals

It's crucial to decide what action you want to take and what kind of result you're after before you can set long-term and short-term goals. To accomplish this effectively, think about taking a current status measurement of a professional function you want to enhance. Then decide on a specific objective based on that knowledge.

For example, you might decide that you want to break the habit of smoking in order to be a role model for your younger siblings. You'll then identify the long term and short-term steps in reaching that specific goal.

Establish a Deadline

Just like developing a routine, setting a deadline for completing objectives can improve the method you use to do immediate activities. Consider writing down each stage of your procedure, along with the estimated amount of time needed to complete each phase, to build a thorough strategy. When making plans, think about going over the procedures to prepare for probable issues and prepare remedies. Your time management abilities will likely increase as a result, which will likely make it simpler to fulfill deadlines.

By keeping note of when and how you finish tasks, you can also create a timetable. This will assist you to re-evaluate and enhance the processes you employ to execute tasks, which can aid in achieving your habit goals.

For instance, if you plan on breaking the habit of procrastination within a year, you can establish weekly deadlines on tasks and objectives that you wish to achieve (that would mostly be interrupted by procrastination). By the time your year is through, you'll have little to no urge of procrastination left.

Specify Benchmarks

A milestone is a relatively small accomplishment that you can use to measure your progress toward a larger objective. Because these enable you to see each step in your goal, and might give you a sense of success if you reach them, milestones could help you focus more. Consider setting a small objective, such as doing a task by a certain date or a lot of chores by a certain time, as a milestone.

For instance, losing 20 pounds with a habit of exercising in six months, might be a milestone for someone. This can enable them to measure their advancement toward their long-term health goal and determine how much time is required to achieve it.

Make Your Objectives SMART Goals

SMART goals are specified, measurable, achievable, relevant, and time-based. Setting SMART objectives can enable you to track your advancement by:

- Creating **specific** goals: Breaking them down into activities might help you comprehend the steps you need to follow to achieve long-term objectives. This will provide you with particular tasks to track. This might also help you come up with a timeframe that would be reasonable for you to attain your objectives.

- Finding out if your objectives are **measurable**: Use time as a metric to make sure your aim is quantifiable. To accomplish this, create a timeline that will help you decide how many activities to complete, how much time to devote to each activity, and how long it might take to reach your overall goal.

- Making sure your objectives are **attainable**: Setting long-term objectives and employing milestones may help you ensure your goals are attainable because some tasks are simpler to do over a longer period of time. Your ability to decide if you need to acquire new skills might be aided by determining how achievable your goals are. Then, by keeping track of the abilities you've acquired and the accomplishments you've made, you can measure your progress.

- Identifying whether your goals are **relevant**: It's useful to assess your goals to make sure they are pertinent before setting them. This might assist you in revising, updating, or changing your goals to make sure they fit your requirements. Additionally, by managing your time better, you'll be able to measure your progress more effectively.

- Developing a **timeline** for your plan of action: By making it easy to see the advancement you've made toward a specific objective, creating a timeline might aid in measuring your progress. This can assist you in establishing reasonable deadlines and updating improbable ones.

Track and Evaluate Advancement

Documenting progress is a useful measurement strategy. Think about writing out your overarching objectives, assignments, deadlines, and milestones for habits. When you accomplish tasks and reach milestones, you may cross them off on a calendar or planner to keep track of your progress. Your planner's information may make it clear to you whether you need to change your timetable or include a new assignment.

In the end, building habits takes more than just intention. But to know how far you've come and assess how far you have to go, will make the process easier. Of course, no one can know when they will break a habit or make a new one, and no one can determine how long self-discipline will last. But being on the top of your game at all times can be an essential tool in your journey, and in the end, you'll look back on the progress you've made and feel proud.

Conclusion

Our habits build us. We are who we are due to our automatic behaviors, and what we do on a regular basis. This is why our productivity, and even our success, depends on our daily decisions and actions. Self-discipline is a driving force in our lives and greatly impacts what we do and how we do it. Hence, self-discipline and habit building and breaking go hand-in-hand.

Having bad habits is natural for humans. We all have instinctive actions that put us at some disadvantage. However, the key action we have to take is to identify these habits and replace them with healthy ones. Healthy habits can improve our productivity, boost our well-being and contribute excessively to our long-term goals. This, along with self-discipline, makes all the difference.

Additionally, the mind is a powerful component of life. Sometimes, we fail to see how much we depend on our immediate thoughts to get through a task or situation. This is why emotions, motivation, willpower and self-control have such a significant impact on our actions and our day-to-day operations. Having emotional intelligence and control is important for self-discipline, since emotions can block our rational thinking and cause us to carry out an action that isn't in line with our ultimate goals. Motivation also acts as a driver to our long-term objectives and is a significant part of habit breaking and building. In the same way, willpower, and self-control work together with self-discipline to determine our actions and decisions, hence, we ought to take control of these, in order to achieve what we truly desire.

It's also important to take care of our physical bodies, since what we do to our bodies affects our minds. Hence, getting the correct nutrients for self-discipline, performing various exercises that add to self-discipline and getting enough rest is vital. These also sometimes lead to healthy habits that we need for our everyday life and well-being.

Another major take-away is our impact on others, and their impact on us. As humans, we are social beings, hence we affect each other directly or indirectly, oftentimes, without even realizing it. We can adopt the habits of those we spend time with, and they can adopt ours. This is why it's important to surround ourselves with highly motivated, positive individuals who will have a beneficial impact on our habits and behaviors, and in turn, we ought to be the very example for others as well. Having role models and being a role model for others, is a significant way to build ourselves and the people around us.

Subsequently, we sometimes confuse habits with routines. Though they are closely related, and routines can lead to habits, routines are more intentional while habits are instinctual. Building healthy routines, nonetheless, has significant benefits on our health, productivity and long-term goals, since they can—and sometimes, inevitably do—lead to habits. Therefore, there are numerous ways in which we can train ourselves to carry out our routines, such as using reminders and triggers. In the same way, establishing rewards for carrying out these routines and habits can be a great and useful way of building motivation to fulfill our goals.

Although there are numerous methods, techniques and skills that influence our behaviors, specific theories and strategies that relate directly to emotions and behavior therapy can be used to help us establish ourselves firmly in good habits and self-discipline. Some of these include Morita Therapy, which can be used to regulate our emotions through the process of building healthy habits, and the Pareto principle, which guides us to input effort into a behavior, which will yield an abundance in results. There is also the If-Then plan, which outlines a formula we can use to rationalize our actions and turn them into habits, and lastly, the Hawthorne Effects, which aims to influence our behavioral habits using subsequent experiments.

In the end, we can then measure our progress by using a variety of tools to ensure we stay on the track of breaking bad habits and replacing them with good habits. Although it won't always be a smooth road, this is essentially vital in the process, since it indicates where we are coming from, and paves the way for a brighter future with better, healthier habits along with grounded self-discipline.

No one wants to have bad habits or have a lack of self-discipline, and good habits are not necessarily far-fetched. We can achieve this with self-discipline, practice, commitment and the right motivational tools. It may not be easy at first, especially if you have a habit that you've been trying to break for years. But with the right techniques and determination, you're right on your way to achieving greatness through your healthy habits.

References

Al-Moussalli, S. (2021, August 11). *The role of family and friends in shaping habits.* Linkedin. https://www.linkedin.com/pulse/role-family-friends-shaping-habits-samaa-al-moussalli-/

Bailey, C. (2018, May 1). *Too lazy to work out, eat well, or save money? Bribe yourself with habit points.* A Life of Productivity. https://alifeofproductivity.com/change-with-habit-points/

Bejelly, K. (2021, December 13). *How nutrition can fuel motivation and ambition.* A Girl Worth Saving. https://agirlworthsaving.net/how-nutrition-can-fuel-motivation-and-ambition/

Businessmirror. (2017, September 21). *Motivation vs self-discipline: Which is the key to habit formation?* https://businessmirror.com.ph/2017/09/21/motivation-vs-self-discipline-which-is-the-key-to-habit-formation/

Cherry, K. (2020, October 13). *The hawthorne effect and behavioral studies.* Very Well Mind. https://www.verywellmind.com/what-is-the-hawthorne-effect-2795234

Cherry, K. (2022, January 26). *How to improve your self-control.* Very Well Mind. https://www.verywellmind.com/psychology-of-self-control-4177125

Davis, T. (n.d). *Habits (good & bad).* Berkeley Well-Being Institute. https://www.berkeleywellbeing.com/habits.html

Fingerprint for Success. (n.d). *How to build self-discipline—even if your willpower is weak.* https://www.fingerprintforsuccess.com/blog/self-discipline#

Fort Behavioral Health. (2020, January 2). *The importance of routines.* https://www.fortbehavioral.com/addiction-recovery-blog/the-importance-of-routines/#:~:text=Routines%20Promote%20Positive%20Self%2DCare,happiness%20and%20feelings%20of%20fulfillment.

Gardner, B., Rebar, A., & Lally, P. (2022). How does habit form? Guidelines for tracking real-world habit formation. *Cogent Psychology*, (9): 1. https://www.tandfonline.com/doi/full/10.1080/23311908.2022.2041277

Ho, L. (2022, April 12). *22 Best habit tracking apps you need in 2022.* Lifehack. https://www.lifehack.org/668261/best-habit-tracking-apps

Ho, L. (2022, May 6). *How to find an accountability partner to help you build habits.* Lifehack. https://www.lifehack.org/862621/accountability-partner

Holden, J.D. (2008). Hawthorne effects and research into professional practice. *Journal of Evaluation in Clinical Practice*, (1), 65-70. https://onlinelibrary.wiley.com/doi/abs/10.1046/j.1365-2753.2001.00280.x

Hyde, E. (2022, June 19). *A simple guide to train yourself to be more self-disciplined.* Management Innovation eXchange. https://www.managementexchange.com/story/simple-guide-train-yourself-be-more-self-disciplined

Indeed Editorial Team. (2021, June 15). *How to measure your progress effectively in 5 steps.* Indeed. https://www.indeed.com/career-advice/career-development/measure-progress

Judah, G., Gardner, B., Kenward, M.G., Destavola, B., & Aunger, R. (2018) Exploratory study of the impact of perceived reward on habit formation. *BMC Psychology*, (6), 62. https://bmcpsychology.biomedcentral.com/articles/10.1186/s40359-018-0270-z#citeas

Kitanishi, K., & Mori, A. (1995). Morita therapy: 1919 to 1995. *Psychiatry and Clinical Neurosciences*, (5-6), 245-254. https://onlinelibrary.wiley.com/doi/abs/10.1111/j.1440-1819.1995.tb01896.x

Laoyan, S. (2022, June 19). *Understanding the Pareto principle (The 80/20 rule).* Asana. https://asana.com/resources/pareto-principle-80-20-rule

Lindley. (2016, February 22). *How your food affects your self-discipline.* All In The Mind. https://www.allinthemind.asia/blog/how-your-food-affects-your-self-discipline

Marano, E. (2003, April 15). *Emotional discipline.* Psychology Today. https://www.psychologytoday.com/us/articles/200304/emotional-discipline

McCarthy, M., Colins, A., Flaherty, S., & McCarthy, S. (2017). Healthy eating habit: A role for goals, identity, and self-control? *Psychology and Marketing,* (8), 772-785. https://onlinelibrary.wiley.com/doi/10.1002/mar.21021

Mayo Clinic Staff. (2022, May 7). *Sleep tips: 6 steps to better sleep.* Mayo Clinic. https://www.mayoclinic.org/healthy-lifestyle/adult-health/in-depth/sleep/art-20048379

Mind Tools Content Team. (n.d). *Managing your emotions at work.* Mind Tools. https://www.mindtools.com/pages/article/newCDV_41.htm

Morita therapy and Japanese psychology. (n.d). Eggshell Therapy and Coaching. https://eggshelltherapy.com/morita/

Newsonen, S. (2015, November 11). *6 Reasons why procrastination can be good for you.* Psychology Today. https://www.psychologytoday.com/us/blog/the-path-passionate-happiness/201511/6-reasons-why-procrastination-can-be-good-you

Participation. (2018, April 18). *Three practical tricks to help you form good habits.* https://www.participaction.com/en-ca/blog/three-practical-tricks-to-help-you-form-good-habits

Rae-Dupree, J. (2008, May 4). *Can you become a creature of new habits?* New York Times. https://www.nytimes.com/2008/05/04/business/04unbox.html#:~:text=Rather%20than%20dismissing%20ourselves%20as,and%20in%20our%20personal%20lives

Robertson, C. (2014, October 29). *The incredible effect of exercise on your willpower.* Willpowered. http://willpowered.com/learn/effects-of-exercise-on-willpower

Robinson, L., Segal, J., & Smith, M. (2021, August). *The mental health benefits of exercise.* Help Guide. https://www.helpguide.org/articles/healthy-living/the-mental-health-benefits-of-exercise.htm

Salzer, S. (2021, April 25). *Your commitment devices database.* Medium. https://medium.com/behavior-design-hub/your-commitment-devices-database-35a54d-f3a64f

Sasson, R. (n.d). *Self discipline benefits and its importance in your life.* Success Consciousness. https://www.successconsciousness.com/blog/inner-strength/self-discipline/

Sasson, R. (n.d.) *Willpower and self discipline exercises and guidance.* Success Consciousness. https://www.successconsciousness.com/blog/inner-strength/willpower-and-self-discipline/

Scott, E. (2022, March 31). *How to deal with negative emotions.* Very Well Mind. https://www.verywellmind.com/how-should-i-deal-with-negative-emotions-3144603

Scott, S. J. (2017, March 4). *155 Ways to reward yourself for reaching your goals.* Develop Good Habits. https://www.developgoodhabits.com/reward-yourself/

Tet. (2018, June 11). *5 Benefits of developing the right habits.* Productive and Free. https://www.productiveandfree.com/blog/benefits-of-habits

Team Ansa. (2022, January 31). *6 steps to create a daily schedule template (with example).* Ansa. https://asana.com/resources/daily-schedule-template

Team Tony. (n.d). *How to surround yourself with good people.* Tony Robbins. https://www.tonyrobbins.com/stories/business-mastery/surround-yourself-with-quality-people/

Tunikova, O. (2019, March 19). *The Science of willpower: How to train your productivity muscle.* Medium. https://medium.com/@tunikova/the-science-of-willpower-how-to-train-your-productivity-muscle-8b2738ce745b

Walker, W. (2020, June 28). *How accountability can help you with self-discipline.* Linkedin. https://www.linkedin.com/pulse/how-accountability-can-help-you-self-discipline-wanda-n-walker/

Wax, D. (2022, February 21). *The importance of reminders (and how to make a reminder work).* Lifehack. https://www.lifehack.org/articles/featured/back-to-basics-reminders.html

Printed in Great Britain
by Amazon

26435552R00079